Green Careers

by Barbara Parks and Jodi Helmer

A member of Penguin Group (USA) Inc.

For my mom and dad, who never questioned why it took countless colleges, cities, and careers to find my passion.
—Jodi

Dedicated to Alexander Michael Ansley Hoy, my 4-year-old grandson, whose innocence and blamelessness ever reminds me that we will be known forever by the tracks we leave.
—Barbara

ALPHA BOOKS

Published by the Penguin Group

Penguin Group (USA) Inc., 375 Hudson Street, New York, New York 10014, USA

Penguin Group (Canada), 90 Eglinton Avenue East, Suite 700, Toronto, Ontario M4P 2Y3, Canada (a division of Pearson Penguin Canada Inc.)

Penguin Books Ltd., 80 Strand, London WC2R 0RL, England

Penguin Ireland, 25 St. Stephen's Green, Dublin 2, Ireland (a division of Penguin Books Ltd.)

Penguin Group (Australia), 250 Camberwell Road, Camberwell, Victoria 3124, Australia (a division of Pearson Australia Group Pty. Ltd.)

Penguin Books India Pvt. Ltd., 11 Community Centre, Panchsheel Park, New Delhi—110 017, India

Penguin Group (NZ), 67 Apollo Drive, Rosedale, North Shore, Auckland 1311, New Zealand (a division of Pearson New Zealand Ltd.)

Penguin Books (South Africa) (Pty.) Ltd., 24 Sturdee Avenue, Rosebank, Johannesburg 2196, South Africa

Penguin Books Ltd., Registered Offices: 80 Strand, London WC2R 0RL, England

Note: This publication contains the opinions and ideas of its authors. It is intended to provide helpful and informative material on the subject matter covered. It is sold with the understanding that the authors and publisher are not engaged in rendering professional services in the book. If the reader requires personal assistance or advice, a competent professional should be consulted.

The authors and publisher specifically disclaim any responsibility for any liability, loss, or risk, personal or otherwise, which is incurred as a consequence, directly or indirectly, of the use and application of any of the contents of this book.

Most Alpha books are available at special quantity discounts for bulk purchases for sales promotions, premiums, fundraising, or educational use. Special books, or book excerpts, can also be created to fit specific needs.

For details, write: Special Markets, Alpha Books, 375 Hudson Street, New York, NY 10014.

Publisher: *Marie Butler-Knight*
Editorial Director: *Mike Sanders*
Senior Managing Editor: *Billy Fields*
Acquisitions Editor: *Tom Stevens*
Development Editor: *Jennifer Bowles*
Senior Production Editor: *Janette Lynn*

Copy Editor: *Megan Wade*
Cover Designer: *Kurt Owens*
Book Designer: *Trina Wurst*
Indexer: *Tonya Heard*
Layout: *Chad Dressler*
Proofreader: *Laura Caddell*

Contents at a Glance

Appendixes

Contents

Introduction

America is hanging out a big help wanted sign: "Wanted: Green workers who can use their education, skills, and experience to save the planet."

The green economy is growing rapidly, reshaping and revitalizing the American economy. Its growth rate is, in fact, higher than the "non-green" economy. As a movement, it has the potential to rival the Industrial Age and the technological revolution, while promising to create a wealth of new opportunities known as *green careers*.

Green careers are, essentially, careers that promote sustainability. Designing a LEED-certified high rise, engineering a new wastewater management system, installing solar panels, and driving a bus that runs on biodiesel are all green careers.

Green careers are available in industries ranging from engineering and environmental activism to agriculture and transportation. The requirements to land a green career are as diverse as the careers themselves, but they do have one thing in common: they're the hottest jobs in the current economy—and the resources to find them are at your fingertips.

How the Book Is Organized

We've made it simple to hone in on the industries that interest you most. Each chapter highlights a different industry and includes a comprehensive list of careers within the field, including the major responsibilities, educational requirements, job growth, and average salaries.

Extras

We've provided lots of extra information to help expand your knowledge of green careers. Look for boxes scattered throughout the chapters that are indicated by their own special icons:

def•i•ni•tion

Look for these boxes to get detailed explanations of the green terms that are included throughout the book.

 Green Guidance

These tips point you in the right direction to launch a green career, regardless of your area of expertise.

Career Crisis
Find out what factors are negatively influencing employment opportunities in various careers.

Inside Scoop
Learn more about trends in the green economy with these valuable nuggets of information.

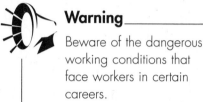

Warning

Beware of the dangerous working conditions that face workers in certain careers.

Acknowledgments

I wish to express thanks to all the attendees of the 2004 Green Festival in San Francisco. It was there, while networking and mingling with 60,000 dedicated, planet-loving individuals, that I felt inspired to "green" my career coaching practice of many years.

Green Career Tracks was founded shortly after with the brainstorming help of my dear friend Kathleen Schuler, children's environmental specialist. I'm grateful for her encouragement to follow my passion and commit to my mission to "support only work and careers that contribute to a more sustainable world."

I'm indebted to many eco-minded individuals who provided information and resources on a wide assortment of green career topics. Special thanks go to Ellen Hopkins, Ecoheart Enterprise; Andres Edwards, EduTracks; all the members of the Northern California Environmental Meetup Group; Jan Hubbard and Doug Shoemaker, Minnesota Renewable Energy Society; and Ami Voeltz, DoItGreen!Minnesota.

Many thanks to Nora Helf, my intern-turned-green-career-specialist, whose exceptional research skills, idea-generating talent, and solid project management skills help keep Green Career Tracks thriving as one of the premier green career services in the United States.

I relied heavily on Jodi Helmer's solid writing and research talents to produce *The Complete Idiot's Guide to Green Careers*. I fully admit I could not, on my own, have pulled this project together in time to meet deadlines.

Working on this book together, we also benefited from our agent Marilyn Allen's uncanny ability to keep the communications and the work process flowing when they might have faltered due to a tight schedule.

Finally, all that I do in the name of writing about or promoting green careers that support a more sustainable world is in gratitude to my clients who keep asking, "Where are the green jobs?"

—Barbara Parks

I suspect that writing a book is a lot like riding in the Tour de France: It takes an entire support team to get one person to the finish line. I'm fortunate to have an amazing team who was with me every step of the way while I was writing this book.

A heartfelt thanks to my agent, Marilyn Allen, for coming to me with this project and navigating all of the bumps along the way. I'm also grateful to my editor, Tom Stevens, who worked with us to develop the content. Your insights were invaluable, and I appreciate the time you took to answer my questions and act as a sounding board during the writing process.

I'm especially thankful to Eric Eckard, researcher extraordinaire, who found obscure stats in a matter of minutes and provided much of the background research I needed to write this book.

A huge thanks to Rebecca Ragain, an amazing friend and green guru, for offering insights throughout the writing process—and for never faltering during all of the last-minute, I-need-help-now requests.

Amanda Cash and Katie DiPaula deserve props for reminding me that even a writer on deadline needs to eat. The home-cooked meals, restaurant outings, and leftovers (not to mention the girl talk) kept me going.

I could not have written a single page of this book without the help of the folks at Coca-Cola who continue to deliver cases of Diet Coke to supermarkets and gas stations in Charlotte, giving me much-needed caffeine boosts to write late into the night.

I'm also incredibly grateful to Molly and Milo for whining until I stepped away from the computer to take them to the park. Sometimes, chasing squirrels is the best way to beat writer's block!

—Jodi Helmer

Trademarks

What, Why, and Where?

In This Chapter

◆ The movement toward a triple bottom line—profits, people, and planet

◆ Legislation that is boosting opportunities in the green economy

◆ A closer look at what defines a green career

◆ Why many green careers are immune to outsourcing

The Need for Green

It's impossible to watch the news, listen to the radio, or read a newspaper without hearing shocking truths about the planet: polar icecaps are melting, rainforests are vanishing, temperatures are rising, acid rain is falling, and pollutants are filling the air. The realization that something needs to be done has led to a global movement to protect the planet.

Al Gore brought green to the mainstream with the release of his Academy Award-winning film *An Inconvenient Truth*, urging everyone to do their part for the environment by driving fuel-efficient vehicles, taking canvas bags to the supermarket, installing low-flow showerheads, and recycling plastic water bottles.

There is no question that a paradigm shift is taking place. In 2007, a poll by the Yale Center for Environmental Law found that the percentage of Americans concerned about global warming reached 84 percent—up from 70 percent in 2004. And, according to a poll conducted by the *Washington Post*, three-quarters of respondents rated the condition of the world's natural environment as fair, poor, or very poor.

As our knowledge about the state of the environment increases, so, too, does our desire to do something about it. It's not just individuals who are taking action: A growing number of companies are making strides to minimize their environmental impacts, emphasizing sustainability as a core business issue and embracing a new, triple bottom line—profit, people, and planet.

The Volvo plant in Sweden has been climate-neutral since 2005; Nike set a goal to be climate-neutral by 2011; and Cisco wants to reduce its greenhouse gas emissions by 25 percent by 2012. In 2007, Xerox met its goal to reduce its greenhouse gas emissions by 10 percent by 2012 and announced a new goal to cut emissions 25 percent by the same date—a 150 percent increase from its original goal.

Google has done its fair share to go green, installing solar panels on the roof of its California headquarters, boosting the efficiencies of its data centers, and maximizing the use of natural light. The tech giant achieved its goal of becoming carbon-neutral in 2007 and is turning its attention toward supporting other environmental projects, committing a total of $30 million to support the research and development of solar and wind power.

In addition to making individual efforts, companies are joining together to encourage change. The U.S. Climate Action Partnership (www.us-cap.org) is a group of 28 companies that are asking the federal government to enact national legislation to require significant reductions in greenhouse gas emissions. To date, member companies include Ford, PepsiCo, General Electric, General Motors, and Shell. Combat Climate Change (www.combatclimatechange.org) is a similar organization. Its 53 member companies, including Citigroup, Hitachi, Reuters, Volvo, and others from around the globe, are pressing for the integration of climate change into world trade markets.

Corporate programs like these are not just helping the environment; they're bolstering the economy. Billions of dollars are being invested in research and development, environmentally friendly legislation, and of course new careers that are turning the need for green into a thriving economic model aimed at safeguarding the future of the planet.

What, Exactly, Is a Green Economy?

The phrase *green economy* is tossed around a lot to describe economic growth that results from investments in environmental initiatives. At its core, the green economy describes a shift toward sustainable business practices, legislation and financial support to bolster environmental programs, and the development of green careers. It's also much more than that—the green economy is a billion-dollar sector of the economy that is growing at a much faster rate than its conventional counterparts, according to Green America (www.coopamerica.org). It's funded by green capital, powered by green technology, and generates green careers.

The green economy is fueled by environmental awareness that is changing the business climate, leading to the restructuring of the global economy into something more sustainable. It encompasses industries ranging from organic produce and alternative fuels to renewable energy and green buildings.

Denmark successfully grew its economy by 50 percent while reducing its greenhouse gas emissions by shifting more of its electricity production to wind energy. China committed to investing $157 billion in environmental protection projects between 2006 and 2010—an investment that equals 1.5 percent of its national gross domestic product. And, Germany has created more than 250,000 new jobs over the past five years in the renewable energy sector alone.

A report issued by the *Environmental Business Journal* (www.ebiusa.com) provided revenue and projected annual growth statistics for 2007–2010 in several sustainable industries:

◆ Resource recovery: $24.13 billion, 15 percent growth

◆ Wastewater treatment: $37.49 billion, 4.6 percent growth

◆ Environmental remediation: $11.55 billion, 4.4 percent growth

◆ Solid waste management: $50.60 billion, 4.2 percent growth

◆ Hazardous waste management: $8.99 billion, 2.2 percent growth

In any sector, growth equals jobs—and the green economy is no exception. Hiring qualified candidates is not as easy as posting help wanted signs, though. The *Environmental Business Journal* report found that "… finding, attracting, recruiting, hiring, training, and retaining qualified people …" is one of the biggest challenges in all sectors of the green economy.

The solution to this challenge? Promoting green careers, funding education and training programs, and providing assistance to help job seekers make the transition to new industries or adjust to the sustainable aspects of their existing fields.

Legislation That's Paving the Way

Government-sponsored programs play an important role in advancing the green economy and increasing the demand for workers in green industries—and there is a lot of legislation that has (or will have) a significant impact. Here's a breakdown of some of the most recent and far-reaching green legislation that's having an impact on the green economy:

- ◆ **The Green Jobs Act (H.R. 2847)**—Authorizes up to $125 million in funding to establish U.S. Department of Labor–administered national and state job training programs to address job shortages in green industries such as energy-efficient construction and building retrofitting, renewable electric power, energy-efficient vehicles, and biofuel development.

- ◆ **The GREEN Act of 2008 (H.R. 6078)**—Encourages energy efficiency; conservation; the development of renewable energy sources for residential, commercial, and industrial buildings; and the creation of sustainable communities.

- ◆ **The Renewable Energy and Job Creation Act of 2008 (H.R. 6049)**—An amendment to the Internal Revenue Code of 1986, it provides $18 billion in tax incentives for investment in renewable energy, carbon capture, energy efficiency, and conservation. It also extends expiring tax provisions and provides individual tax relief for other purposes.

- ◆ **The Energy Independence and Security Act of 2007 (H.R. 6)**—Calls for increased production of clean renewable fuels and increased efficiency of products, buildings, and vehicles. This act promotes research on greenhouse gas capture and storage options and improvement of the energy performance of the federal government, with a goal of moving the United States toward greater energy independence and security.

- ◆ **H.R. 6566**—Aimed at increasing the safe, domestic production and development of alternative and renewable energy, it also promotes conservation.

◆ **Executive Order 13423**—Requires federal agencies to conduct their environmental, transportation, and energy-related activities in environmentally, economically, and fiscally sound and sustainable manners. It sets specific targets, including improving energy efficiency and reducing greenhouse gas emissions of individual agencies through the reduction of energy intensity by 3 percent per year through 2015, or 30 percent by the end of fiscal year 2015, compared to energy use in 2003.

◆ **The Energy Policy Act of 2005 (Executive Order 13423)**—A Department of Energy (DOE) initiative to reduce energy intensity across the nationwide DOE complex by 30 percent. Actions might include installing onsite renewable energy projects or operating the entire fleet of vehicles exclusively on alternative fuels.

The Green Job Market: What Is It, and How Can You Get Involved?

The green job market is one of the most talked about aspects of the green economy, but defining it is difficult: There is almost unanimous agreement that green careers provide fair wages, good benefits, opportunities for advancement, and healthy working conditions and are accessible to job seekers from all backgrounds in all areas of the country. There is almost no accepted standard, however, when it comes to agreeing on the specific industries and responsibilities that define a green career.

Miners who extract coke that is transformed into steel and used to build wind turbines have green jobs, right? What about miners who extract coke that is transformed into steel that is used to make SUVs?

The differing end results make it impossible, based on the job title alone, to decide whether mining is considered a green career. So, a broader definition is needed.

The green job market can include all industries and job titles as long as a few criteria are met. Green careers must have environmental benefits, such as reducing waste or pollution, supporting renewable energy, researching sustainable technologies, safeguarding natural resources, or repairing environmental damage. Opportunities in green careers are expanding at a rapid pace as a result of local, state, and federal programs aimed at boosting opportunities in the green economy.

The Green Jobs for America Campaign is a national campaign to educate the public about the need for investments in green jobs. It is spearheaded by the Sierra Club, the Blue Green Alliance, United Steelworkers, the Natural Resources Defense Council (NRDC), and the Center for American Progress and Green for All. To date, the program is at work in 12 states—Florida, Indiana, Minnesota, Missouri, Nebraska, New York, Ohio, Oregon, Pennsylvania, Tennessee, Virginia, and Wisconsin—to promote the creation of green jobs.

The Million Solar Roofs Initiative (www.millionsolarroofs.org) set a goal of promoting the installation of one million solar roofs across the United States by 2010, creating approximately 70,000 green careers in the process.

In 2006 alone, the American Solar Energy Society (www.ases.org) estimated that the renewable energy and energy efficiency industries were responsible for $970 billion in revenues and 8.5 million jobs—a number that the Society expects to grow exponentially as the United States solidifies its commitment to reducing carbon emissions and improving energy efficiency.

The green job market has created new industries, new jobs, and new responsibilities within existing jobs. Now, careers that were once unheard of, including sustainability managers, climate change analysts, Leadership in Energy and Environmental Design (LEED) consultants, wind energy engineers, and EcoBrokers, are common occupations that have become part of the global vocational vocabulary.

So, what does it take to get involved in the green job market?

In some ways, finding a green career is the same as looking for any job. It requires researching companies, scouring the want ads and online job postings, joining professional associations, writing resumes and cover letters, scheduling informational interviews, attending career fairs, and (hopefully) negotiating multiple job offers.

Sometimes, landing a green career is about searching for jobs with sustainable-sounding titles, such as "conservationist," "environmental engineer," or "green roof designer." Green careers can be lurking behind the wheel of a hybrid vehicle or inside a LEED-certified building. To this end, it's important to investigate a company's environmental policies: Is it working to reduce its carbon footprint? Does it have a comprehensive recycling program in place? Are efforts in place to reduce energy? Is the company accessible by public transportation?

The Carbon Disclosure Project (www.cdproject.net) is a good place to start. The website offers details of the greenhouse gas emissions of some of the largest companies in the world. Currently, 1,300 companies are participating. Information about a company's green initiatives is also available on corporate websites and during interviews; some companies are even publishing sustainability reports that provide comprehensive information about their efforts to green operations.

Armed with information about sustainable industries and eco-friendly companies, all that's left to do is to start searching for a great green career.

Market Outlook for Green Careers

One of the biggest challenges for corporations is also one of the biggest opportunities for job seekers—the shortage of skilled workers needed to fill the abundance of new careers created by the growing green economy.

A survey conducted by the National Association of Manufacturers (www.nam.org) found that 90 percent of respondents reported a moderate to severe shortage of qualified workers. The National Renewable Energy Laboratory (www.nrel.gov) reports that a shortage of skills and training is the leading barrier to improving renewable energy and energy efficiency.

Every day, new programs are launched to promote the growth of the green economy: Washington, D.C., has implemented a green-collar job-training program; New York enacted the Green Procurement and Agency Sustainability Program to reduce materials and energy consumption; and Massachusetts has signed a global warming law that requires reducing greenhouse gas emissions to 80 percent below 1990 levels by 2050. Additionally, the Apollo Alliance (www.apolloalliance.org), a coalition of business, labor, environmental, and community leaders promoting environmental change, has proposed $300 billion in federal funding over the next decade to support green projects that would lead to the creation of approximately 3 million new green careers.

One of the oft-touted benefits of green careers is their immunity to outsourcing. It's virtually impossible to perform an energy audit, install solar panels, lead outdoor education classes, drive hybrid buses, or manage recycling centers from overseas.

Right now, there is a shortage of workers needed to fill the jobs created by the green economy, according to UPI Energy Watch (www.upi.com), and the demand for workers in green industries continues to grow, making it a great time to start exploring green careers.

Chapter 2

Environment

In This Chapter

- ◆ The environmental consulting career, which is poised for explosive growth

- ◆ More than 382,000 new jobs for college professors expected by 2016

- ◆ Possible hiring incentives for science teachers

- ◆ Continuing education classes aimed at helping political lobbyists raise awareness of environmental causes

- ◆ Fundraising careers that support the green efforts of nonprofit organizations

The task of safeguarding the environment doesn't fall on a single profession. Instead, it takes workers from a range of industries to raise environmental awareness, bolster corporate environmental responsibility, support green legislation, raise funds to support environmental programs, and educate the next generation of environmental stewards.

Career opportunities in environmental consulting, education, law, and nonprofit and corporate management are growing at much faster rates than careers in other industries. The field of environmental protection and preservation is one where the responsibilities, educational requirements, and pay scales are as varied as the job titles. Regardless of the industry, this field has some of the most sought-after green careers.

Environmental Analysis/Consulting

Environmental consulting is a $125 billion industry, according to the *Environmental Business Journal*, with the number of firms growing more than 26 percent between 2001 and 2006. The demand for environmental analysis and consulting has exploded, making it one of the largest specialties in scientific and technical consulting services. Along with tremendous growth in the industry comes a demand for professionals to provide analysis and consulting services. The jobs in this field didn't exist a decade ago, but demand has created new opportunities in the green economy.

Climate Change Analyst

Climate change analysts study climate, weather patterns, and natural disasters to help businesses, nonprofit organizations, and government agencies create plans for adapting to climate change. Their job duties can include projecting carbon emissions, conducting market and risk analyses for energy supply technologies, evaluating public policy options, and writing technical reports.

Inside Scoop

In 2008, the Pew Center on Global Climate Change (www.pewclimate.org) released *Adapting to Climate Change: A Business Approach* to outline the risks—and possible opportunities, including the creation of new jobs—that businesses face as a result of climate change. You can download the entire report at www.pewclimate.org/business-adaptation.

Climate change analysts provide insights to help clients adapt to current and possible future greenhouse gas regulations and emissions trading programs, assess resource availability, and adjust business processes. In some cases, climate change analysts help shape policies relating to climate change, participating in legislative hearings, policy briefings, and shareholder meetings.

Working as a climate change analyst requires a master's degree in climatology, geography, environmental science, or public policy. A Ph.D. in a similar discipline improves job opportunities.

The Association for the Advancement of Science (www.aaas.org) is working to expand opportunities for scientific leadership on the issue of climate change. To this end, the association provides research reports, job listings, and annual meetings on issues relating to science and the environment, including climate change.

The median annual salary for a climate change analyst is $72,408.

Carbon Management Consultant

Carbon management consultants are responsible for helping clients reduce their *carbon footprints*. Their duties might include performing *carbon audits*, identifying energy efficiency improvements, assessing renewable energy options, advising on green building upgrades, suggesting eco-friendly suppliers, implementing green communication options, and promoting carbon-neutral business travel. To do their jobs, carbon management consultants often partner with energy auditors, architects, landscape designers, and other contractors to perform assessments and develop sustainable design and building improvement plans.

def•i•ni•tion

A **carbon footprint** measures the amount of carbon dioxide and other greenhouse gases emitted by a person, corporation, or lifecycle of a product or service. It was designed to help conceptualize the amount of personal and/or organizational impact on global warming.

Carbon audits are used to measure the carbon footprints of organizations for the purposes of carbon emissions trading.

Some companies have in-house carbon management consultants, but most of these professionals work for small firms that specialize in developing carbon management plans.

The job market for carbon management consultants is expected to double in 2008, and increase to 50 times its current size by 2012, making it one of the fastest-growing segments in the corporate environmental sector.

A carbon management consultant needs a bachelor's degree in engineering, environmental science, or a related field; a graduate degree is beneficial. The Norwich Business School at the University of East Anglia (www.uea.ac.uk) in England began offering an MBA in strategic carbon management in 2008. It's billed as the first and only MBA of its kind in the world.

The average salary for a carbon management consultant is $124,200 per year.

Air and Water Quality Technician

Air and water quality technicians oversee projects related to air and water quality. They might perform tests to ensure that drinking water meets government standards, monitor carbon dioxide levels near landfills, or analyze the environmental effects of wastewater.

The daily responsibilities can include air and water testing and sampling, conducting technical evaluations, preparing impact analyses, and designing programs to improve air and water quality. Air and water quality technicians work with clients such as factories and industrial plants to develop comprehensive plans that ensure that the requirements of the *Clean Air Act* and the *Clean Water Act*—acts that set the standards for the United States—are met.

def•i•ni•tion

The **Clean Air Act** sets limits on how much of a pollutant can be in the air. It was amended in 1990 to include provisions for addressing acid rain, ozone depletion, and toxic air pollution. It also established a national permits program and proposed emissions trading.

The **Clean Water Act** enacts standards for water pollution, including reducing water pollution from industrial facilities, governments, and agricultural operations. It was enacted in 1977 to set allowable pollutant levels for water bodies such as rivers, lakes, streams, and wetlands.

Most air and water quality technicians work for engineering and consulting firms, corporations, state and federal governments, and in some cases nonprofit organizations.

The job requires a bachelor's degree in environmental science, engineering, or a related field. Advanced certification and membership in professional associations can improve job opportunities.

The Water Quality Association (www.wqa.org) offers several areas of accreditation, including Certified Water Specialist. The association also posts job listings on its website and hosts an annual conference. The Air & Waste Management Association (www.awma.org) offers professional development courses in air pollution, validating air toxics data, ozone depleting substance regulations, and air emissions inventories.

The Institute of Clean Air Companies (www.icac.com) also maintains a comprehensive list of job openings in the field.

The median salary for an air and water quality technician is $48,400 per year.

Stormwater Engineer

Stormwater engineers develop solutions for managing stormwater. Their duties can include planning low-impact residential and commercial developments, designing stormwater conveyance systems, supporting habitat restoration and redesign, and devising appropriate structures for stormwater detention and water quality treatment. Stormwater engineers may also participate in policy development for stormwater management.

def•i•ni•tion

Stormwater is the flow of water that results from precipitation such as rain and snow. Stormwater soaks into the surface of the soil, saturates plants, and evaporates into the atmosphere. The stormwater that remains becomes runoff and has a serious impact on the environment. Runoff can cause erosion of land area and stream banks, increase flooding, and carry pollutants to surface waters. Increased development destroys natural areas and results in more runoff.

The increasing concern over stormwater management has created opportunities for stormwater engineers to devise new, environmentally friendly strategies for managing runoff. In addition to traditional means of managing runoff, stormwater engineers may also use green roofs, permeable pavements, water harvesting systems, and stormwater wetlands to help minimize the environmental impact of runoff.

Stormwater engineers often work for engineering or architectural firms, although jobs are available with government agencies, public utilities, and nonprofit organizations. The job often involves working in the field, studying the problems, analyzing the effectiveness of any existing stormwater management systems, and working with a team of engineers and architects to devise practical and environmentally friendly solutions.

Stormwater engineers need a minimum of a bachelor's degree in civil engineering, environmental engineering, or a related field. Most companies also look for candidates with a Professional Engineering (PE) designation. A master's degree in an engineering discipline can improve employment opportunities.

The National Association of Flood & Stormwater Management Agencies (www. nafsma.org) hosts annual meetings and networking events, and provides updates on the latest stormwater-related news. Most states also have regional stormwater associations.

The average salary for a stormwater engineer is $66,000 per year.

Geographic Information Systems Specialist

Geographic information systems (GIS) specialists use software programs to create and maintain data, including maps, to provide details on transportation networks, land use boundaries, environmental areas, and information about existing infrastructure. Their duties include creating maps and graphs using GIS software, gathering and integrating data, and analyzing geographic relationships among different types of data. GIS specialists may gather data from field observation, satellite imagery, aerial photographs, and existing maps. The job also entails creating reports, presenting information to end users, and answering questions about the data.

> **Inside Scoop**
>
> In Southern California, GIS mapping helped boost support for the protection of 81,000 hectares of desert habitat. GIS specialists created maps that illustrated the projected results of development over time that helped earn public and governmental support for managing development.

The data provided by GIS specialists is used to make decisions about land use planning, the impact on natural resources, and the protection of wildlife. In the field, GIS specialists can map areas to evaluate their risk for fire and assess the health of rangelands to determine the suitability of an area as a wildlife habitat. Other uses for GIS mapping include showing changes in an environment over time and mapping transportation infrastructure to assist in planning for mass transit expansion.

Most GIS specialists work for government agencies or utilities. Positions are also available in engineering and consulting firms. GIS specialists may also be self-employed as consultants, updating and evaluating data or assisting businesses with GIS-related technical needs. The job does require some fieldwork, although GIS specialists spend most of their time in an office setting.

GIS specialists need a bachelor's degree in geographic information systems, photogrammetry, geography, or a related field. A master's degree can improve employment opportunities.

Career Crisis
The use of GIS is on the rise, but it might not lead to more career opportunities for GIS specialists. Instead, those working as drafters, cartographers, and environmental engineers may be required to add GIS mapping and analysis to their existing job duties.

There are several professional associations that provide information and support to GIS specialists. The American Society for Photogrammetry and Remote Sensing (www.asprs.org) offers numerous accreditation programs, including Certified Mapping Scientist and Certified GIS Technologist as well as conferences, professional development opportunities, and job postings. The Association of American Geographers (www.aag.org) and the University Consortium for Geographic Information Science (www.ucgis.org) also offer networking opportunities, educational programs, and special events to members.

GIS specialists earn an average salary of $62,345 per year.

Environmental Education

The next generation of green-collar workers and environmental advocates is eager to learn about the environment. Educators are armed with the knowledge to teach lessons about the research, science, and rationale for protecting the environment.

Careers in environmental education are available at all levels, from teaching kindergarten children songs about the planet to lecturing graduate students about the possibilities of geothermal energy. Right now, the demand for environmental educators is outpacing almost all other sectors of the green economy.

College Professor

College professors prepare lectures, lead seminars, and oversee lab experiments. In the course of their work, college professors, also called faculty, develop curriculum, grade exams, advise students, and supervise teaching assistants.

A growing number of colleges are offering green degrees in subjects ranging from environmental engineering and wastewater management to sustainable design and eco-friendly investing. These programs combine core curricula for a degree program with focused instruction on environmental topics and offer more opportunities for college professors who specialize in these fields.

Most college professors combine classroom instruction with research in their areas of expertise. College professors specializing in environmental topics might spend part of the academic term in the field, conducting research on topics ranging from air quality and habitat restoration to erosion and emissions trading.

Inside Scoop

At some colleges, professors will be doing more than just teaching green classes; they'll be working on green campuses. The Association for the Advancement of Sustainability in Higher Education (www.aashe.org) is a member organization of colleges and universities in the United States and Canada that is working to promote sustainability in higher education. Its goal is to green all aspects of campus operations from governance to curriculum and outreach.

The National Center for Education Statistics (www.nces.ed.gov) expects college enrollment to increase 14 percent by 2016, reaching a record level of 18 million. Increased enrollment, coupled with the growing number of degree programs, has created a strong job market for college professors. According to the Bureau of Labor Statistics (BLS), opportunities are expected to increase 23 percent by 2016, leading to the creation of 382,000 new jobs—among the largest number of new jobs in any industry.

Most colleges require professors to have a Ph.D., although it is possible to secure a teaching position with a master's degree.

The American Association of University Professors (www.aaup.org) provides the latest news and research on all aspects of teaching at the post-secondary level.

College professors earn a median annual salary of $56,120.

Outdoor Educator

Outdoor educators develop programs that focus on learning about the outdoors. Lessons can include guided nature hikes that focus on local flora and fauna, classroom sessions about animals that live in wetlands, games that explore fun facts about the outdoors, or lectures on the impacts of global warming. Their overall goal is to teach people about nature and encourage them to experience the natural world.

Outdoor educators participate in conservation efforts, coordinate volunteers to assist with preservation activities, create promotional materials for outdoor educational programs, and might act as media spokespeople on various environmental topics.

Inside Scoop

The Chesapeake Bay Foundation (www.cbf.org) founded the No Child Left Inside Coalition to promote outdoor education. The 600-member organization is seeking federal legislation to provide funding for environmental education. If passed, funds would support outdoor learning activities, teacher training, and environmental literacy plans, leading to more job opportunities for outdoor educators.

National forests, state parks, nature preserves, recreation centers, and nonprofits are some of the organizations that hire outdoor educators. The job can involve working evenings and weekends. Outdoor educators often work for outdoor education centers and are required to live onsite. In these settings, the job duties often include helping with meals and assisting with site management, including gardening and light maintenance, in exchange for room and board.

The educational requirements for outdoor educators are varied. Some employers prefer candidates with a bachelor's degree in environmental science or a related field, whereas others require a high school diploma.

The Association for Environmental and Outdoor Education (www.aeoe.org) provides job listings, educational resources, and annual conferences relating to the field of outdoor education.

The median annual salary for an outdoor educator is $17,110.

Science Teacher

Science teachers teach classes in science disciplines such as chemistry, biology, and physics. They create lesson plans, design tests and experiments, grade homework, and evaluate student performance. Science teachers also plan field trips, schedule guest speakers, coordinate science fairs, and assist with science-related extracurricular activities.

Green Guidance

School districts across the United States are facing severe shortages of science teachers, according to the National Academy of Sciences (www.nasonline.org). To attract new science teachers, some states have instituted alternative certification programs that allow college graduates to postpone teacher certification to enter the classroom immediately. Several districts have even begun offering financial incentives such as signing bonuses, student loan forgiveness, housing assistance, and tuition reimbursement to boost teacher recruitment.

Science teachers play an important role in teaching students about the environment. Their curriculum can include lessons about the causes of global warming, the impact of pollution on wildlife, and the importance of preserving wetlands. It's essential for science teachers to use creative and age-appropriate materials to educate students. Lessons for middle school students can include games and field trips. In high school, science teachers might show documentaries and assign research projects.

Currently, there are 4 million teachers in the United States. The BLS estimates that an additional 479,000 teaching positions will become available by 2016, with special emphasis on recruiting math and science teachers.

Science teachers need a bachelor's degree with a science major such as chemistry, biology, or physics, as well as a license from the State Board of Education.

Several professional associations are designed to provide teaching support, continuing education, and job postings to science teachers. The largest associations include the National Science Teachers Association (www.nsta.org), the National Earth Science Teachers Association (www.nestanet.org), the National Association of Biology Teachers (www.nabt.org), and the American Association of Physics Teachers (www.aapt.org).

The median salary for a science teacher is $48,690 per year.

Environmental Law

Careers in environmental law put professionals on the front lines of environmental protection, promoting legislation that helps safeguard the environment and ensures that environmental mismanagement is punished. It's a demanding field that requires advanced education, long hours, and intense dedication. However, the payoff—earning a living by protecting the environment—is worth the effort.

Lawyer

Lawyers conduct research, prepare legal briefs, provide legal advice, and represent clients in court. The specific job duties lawyers perform vary depending on their areas of specialization. Lawyers who work in private practice concentrate on criminal or civil law. Criminal lawyers represent clients who have been charged with crimes, whereas civil lawyers assist clients with contracts, litigations, wills, mortgages, and other legal documents.

Environmental law is a growing area of specialization. Lawyers in this field are responsible for enforcing laws that protect the environment and punishing actions that are harmful. In this role, lawyers might draft legislation to protect wetlands on behalf of special interest groups, provide legal advice to corporations on complying with environmental regulations, and prosecuting environmental offenders.

There are approximately 761,000 lawyers in the United States. Opportunities for environmental lawyers are expected to increase 25 percent in the next decade, according to the Boston-based consulting firm Green Economy.

Lawyers might work for law firms, legal aid societies, nonprofit organizations, or various levels of government as attorneys general, prosecutors, and public defenders. Some lawyers are employed by corporations as house counsel, advising companies on legal issues related to business activities such as patents, contracts, government regulations, or collective bargaining agreements.

> ### Inside Scoop
>
> The National Environmental Policy Act was passed in 1970 to form policies to protect the environment. Its purpose is to force governmental agencies to consider the effects of their decisions on the environment and has been described as one of the most far-reaching environmental legislation ever passed.

A lawyer must complete law school to earn a law degree, called a juris doctorate (J.D.) that allows her to practice law. Law school applicants must have a bachelor's degree and take the Law School Admission Test (LSAT). Upon graduation, lawyers have to register with their state bar, which requires passing a written exam. Currently, law school graduates in 52 jurisdictions are required to pass the Multistate Professional Responsibility Examination (MPRE), which tests their knowledge of American Bar Association codes on professional responsibility and judicial conduct.

The Environmental Law Institute (www.eli.org) offers seminars and boot camps on environmental law to members, focusing on emerging issues in law and practice.

The median salary for lawyers is $102,470 per year.

Lobbyist

Lobbyists work to influence legislative matters, often on behalf of special interest groups, constituents, or other legislators. Their roles can include studying proposed legislation to determine its impact, launching advertising campaigns to sway decision-makers, contacting elected officials to persuade them to support specific legislation, and testifying at public hearings.

There are two main types of lobbyists: those who approach politicians directly to influence their opinions and those who work through grassroots organizations to further their causes.

Lobbyists who specialize in environmental causes can try to earn support for legislation that protects the environment or assist nonprofit organizations to introduce bills that further their missions. Approximately 19,000 registered lobbyists work in Washington, according to the Legislative Resource Center (www.clerk.house.gov).

A minimum of a bachelor's degree is required to work as a lobbyist. Many lobbyists have graduate degrees, typically in law or public policy. The Public Affairs and Advocacy Institute (www.spa.american.edu) offers continuing education courses such as The Art and Craft of Lobbying, and Lobbying Rules and Regulations. The organization also offers a two-week workshop on professional lobbying twice a year. The American League of Lobbyists (www.alldc.org) offers a lobbying certificate program.

The median annual salary for a lobbyist is $49,060.

Legislative Analyst

Legislative analysts provide nonpartisan reports on the impact of proposed legislation, analyze ballot measures, conduct public policy research, and review state budgets. They can also contact advocacy groups, attend policy committee meetings, participate on governmental task forces, and recruit citizens to serve on committees.

Legislative analysts need a bachelor's degree in political science, public policy, or business administration.

The National Association of Legislative Fiscal Offices (www.ncsl.org/nalfo) is an association of legislative staff focused on fiscal research and analysis. The American Political Science Association (www.apsanet.org) offers continuing education, job listings, networking opportunities, and fellowships for those in political science careers (including legislative analysts).

Legislative analysts earn a median salary of $51,981 per year.

Corporate Environmental Management

Corporations are often seen as environmental enemies, mismanaging resources, polluting, and putting profits before environmental protection. In some cases, the reputation is well deserved, but some companies are working hard to do the right thing. The approach? Hiring green career professionals to help reduce their environmental impact and spread the word about corporate green initiatives. The field of corporate environmental management combines new careers with tried-and-true professions that have taken on a green twist.

Sustainability Manager

Sustainability managers oversee corporate environmental programs. Their goal is to formalize a corporation's commitment to the environment. To this end, sustainability managers develop policies for corporate environmental responsibility, evaluate decisions based on financial and sustainability goals, and advise employees on making decisions with environmental best practices in mind. The job can also entail conducting research on sustainability trends and providing educational opportunities for employees.

On a daily basis, sustainability managers might calculate corporate carbon footprints; develop new relationships with green suppliers; and communicate a corporation's environmental message to clients, employees, and stakeholders.

Sustainability managers need a bachelor's degree; some companies might even require candidates to have a graduate degree.

The International Society of Sustainability Professionals (www.sustainabilityprofessionals.org) offers continuing education courses aimed at sustainability professionals.

The median salary for a sustainability manager is $68,020 per year.

Public Relations Specialist

Public relations specialists manage internal and external communications for businesses, nonprofits, associations, educational institutions, and other organizations. Their role is to develop communications strategies, prepare marketing materials, and act as media spokespeople. The daily responsibilities of a public relations specialist include drafting press releases and contacting members of the media to publicize their message; preparing speeches for executives; responding to inquiries from the public, media, and other organizations; and coordinating special events.

Green Guidance

A growing number of public relations firms are specializing in green PR to help companies spread their environmental messages. Public relations specialists who want to focus on green PR and prefer to work for agencies that represent multiple clients can seek opportunities with these firms.

In companies that want to promote a certain environmental message, public relations specialists—also called communication coordinators, press secretaries, and information officers—ensure that the information gets widespread attention. They might speak to the media about the threat of global warming or the benefits of drought-tolerant landscaping. Their job is also to highlight their organization's efforts to go green by publicizing environmental awards and achievements.

Some public relations specialists work a 40-hour week, whereas others frequently work overtime, including evenings and weekends. In some organizations, public relations specialists can be on call around the clock.

Employment for public relations specialists is expected to increase 18 percent by 2016. The BLS predicts that contract positions at public relations firms will make up the fastest-growing segment of the industry.

Entry-level positions require a bachelor's degree in public relations, communication, journalism, or a related field. A master's degree is recommended, especially for senior positions.

The Public Relations Society of America (www.prsa.org) offers an Accredited in Public Relations designation to members. To earn the designation, members need a bachelor's degree and/or significant work experience in the field and must pass a written exam.

The International Association of Business Communicators (www.iabc.com) hosts conferences and networking events for communications professionals. The association also offers the Accredited Business Communicator designation. Candidates must have a bachelor's degree and at least five years of experience in the field; they are also required to submit a portfolio of work samples and pass written and oral exams.

The median annual salary for a public relations specialist is $47,350.

Nonprofit Environmental Management

Nonprofit organizations get a lot of press for their efforts to protect the environment. Established nonprofits such as the Audubon Society and Greenpeace are working alongside grassroots environmental organizations that have sprung up across the country with a similar goal: to raise funds and deliver programs to protect the environment.

In 1995, there were just 24,000 nonprofit environmental groups in the United States, with $14 billion in assets. In 2008, that number jumped to more than 34,000 groups with more than $38 billion in assets. More organizations and more funding means more opportunities in environmental nonprofit management.

Development Director

Development directors oversee all fundraising efforts for nonprofit organizations. It's their job to establish fundraising goals and implement programs to reach those goals. To do this, development directors coordinate capital campaigns, write grant proposals, develop corporate giving partnerships, and make appeals to individual donors. Depending on the size of the organization, development directors might also assist with special events; write thank-you letters to donors; and supervise staff, interns, and volunteers.

Development directors work for nonprofit organizations, professional associations, and civic groups where their fundraising efforts help to support operating costs, staff salaries, and programs offered by the organization. In green nonprofits, the funds raised by development directors might be used to launch public awareness campaigns about environmental issues, lobby for pro-environment legislation, fund alternative energy projects, or develop community gardening programs.

Inside Scoop

Charitable gifts in the United States topped $306 billion in 2007, according to Giving USA, a report produced by Chicago-based consulting firm Campbell & Company (www.campbellcompany.com). Individual contributions accounted for more than 82 percent of donations; foundations made up 12 percent; and corporations accounted for 5 percent of total gifts.

The BLS expects opportunities for development directors to increase 14.6 percent by 2016, creating upwards of 20,000 new jobs.

Most development directors are employed by agencies with five or fewer staff members. They often work evenings and weekends to attend special events, and the job can require frequent travel to meet with supporters and potential donors.

The minimum requirement for a career as a development director is a bachelor's degree in business administration, nonprofit management, or a related field. National organizations with multimillion-dollar operating budgets require development directors to have a graduate degree.

The Association of Fundraising Professionals (www.afpnet.org) offers the Certified Fund Raising Executive designation as well as annual conferences, fundraising resources, networking opportunities, and job listings to members.

Development directors earn a median annual salary of $76,770.

Program Manager

Program managers oversee all aspects of a specific program within a nonprofit organization. Their role is to set goals and objectives, oversee program implementation, manage promotion and participant recruitment, and conduct evaluations. They might also recruit and train volunteers.

Program managers can oversee a range of programs, from low-income housing assistance and equal access to medical care to granting wishes for terminally ill children and conducting spay-and-neuter programs. In nonprofit organizations that focus on environmental causes, program managers might coordinate efforts to protect endangered species, preserve wildlife refuges, promote water conservation, and support outdoor education.

In most cases, program managers need a bachelor's degree, although some organizations will hire program managers with a high school diploma and experience in a nonprofit setting. Interns and volunteers are often excellent candidates for program management positions.

The Center for Nonprofit Management (www.cnm.org) offers a Nonprofit Leadership Development Program aimed at helping senior staff improve their nonprofit management skills. The center also hosts special events and provides resources on nonprofit management.

The Alliance for Nonprofit Management (www.allianceonline.org) provides assistance to help nonprofits meet their goals. Program managers can benefit from technical assistance, educational programs, grants, and technology solutions.

The median salary for a program manager is $38,445 per year.

Canvasser

Canvassers solicit donations from individuals, often through door-to-door appeals or phone campaigns. Canvassers might also attend community events to collect signatures and donations in support of environmental initiatives.

Canvassers play an important role in nonprofit fundraising efforts. In addition to raising funds, canvassers also help spread the word about causes and organizations that are on the forefront of the environmental movement.

Shifts in the evenings and on weekends are common, and canvassers often work part-time. In some cases, canvassers have full-time jobs in other fields but take on this role as a means of supporting a favorite organization or cause.

There are no formal educational requirements to work as a canvasser. Instead, organizations look for canvassers who have excellent communication skills and are knowledgeable about the issues they're discussing with prospective donors.

The median wage for a canvasser is $6.55 per hour.

Green Building

In This Chapter

- ◆ An overview of the green building industry
- ◆ The most popular green building jobs
- ◆ New job opportunities created by the skyrocketing demand for green buildings
- ◆ Job prospects for Leadership in Energy and Environmental Design Accredited Professionals
- ◆ A new certification program for green roof designers

Green building is a hot topic. The idea that building green homes, skyscrapers, office buildings, and industrial plants is a surefire way to protect the planet has caused a huge increase in investment in green building and design. In fact, the National Association of Homebuilders reports that green building will be a $50 billion market by 2010.

The increased demand for green building is creating job opportunities in all sectors of the green building industry. Construction workers, skilled tradesmen, urban planners, energy auditors, consultants, and designers are all taking advantage of opportunities to secure green-collar jobs that are as healthy for their pocketbooks as they are for the environment.

Land Use/Planning

The success of green building starts from the ground up—literally. The most sustainable construction projects include comprehensive plans for land use that reduces the use of natural resources, minimizes ecosystem destruction, and curtails pollution.

Workers in land use and planning industries play a significant role in environmental protection by carefully assessing site selection, planning for future growth, attempting responsible redevelopment of contaminated sites, and controlling erosion and pollution. The environmental impact of these careers is most notable in urban areas. Currently, cities are responsible for up to 75 percent of worldwide energy use and up to 80 percent of greenhouse gas emissions. In these careers, the environmental stakes are high, and so are the opportunities and salaries for skilled workers.

Urban Planner

Urban planners develop strategies for land use and growth in urban, suburban, and rural communities. An urban planner's role is to formulate plans for development by consulting on the best use of land and resources, assessing land use compatibility, making recommendations for the design and placement of infrastructure, and suggesting zoning regulations. In the course of their daily activities, urban planners consider environmental issues such as sustainable development, air pollution, traffic congestion, and land values.

Urban planners are also key players in urban renewal efforts, adapting planning methods to revitalize inner cities and rundown neighborhoods where infrastructure has deteriorated.

Urban planners can work for local governments, cities, counties, engineering firms, developers, and private property owners. Their services can be used to develop plans for public and private housing, commercial development, public facilities such as parks and libraries, public transportation, community redevelopment, and master-planned communities.

A growing number of urban planners are also involved in environmental issues, including pollution control, wetland preservation, and forest conservation. In some cases, urban planners might also be called on to help draft legislation on environmental issues.

Widespread interest in *sustainable urban development* has created new opportunities for urban planners who want to focus their efforts on lessening the environmental impact of development.

def•i•ni•tion

Sustainable urban development aims to improve the long-term social and environmental health of cities. It includes compact land use (the practice of including more development in less space), improved access to public transportation, efficient resource use, decreased pollution and waste, restoration of the natural environment, sustainable economics, preservation of local culture, and community involvement.

Several specialized disciplines exist within urban planning. Planners can choose to focus on regional, transportation, housing, community, or environmental planning.

A minimum of a bachelor's degree is required to secure a position as an urban planner. To advance within the field (and to pursue employment with most government agencies), a master's degree in urban or regional planning is necessary. The American Institute of Certified Planners (www.planning.org/aicp) offers urban planners additional accreditation that can provide an edge when searching for a job. Currently, New Jersey is the only state that requires urban planners to be licensed.

Approximately 68 percent of the 34,000 urban planners in the United States work for local governments. Job opportunities for urban planners are expected to grow 15 percent by 2016, with the largest number of jobs in the private sector, primarily in the professional, scientific, and technical services industries.

The average annual salary for an urban planner is $56,630.

Environmental Site Assessor

An environmental site assessor prepares comprehensive technical reports about potential contamination of a prospective building site. The documentation that an environmental assessor prepares also contains information about nearby hazardous sites, which an environmental site assessor must investigate as part of developing a comprehensive research report.

On a day-to-day basis, an environmental site assessor might measure and observe substances in the air, water, and soil for signs of contamination that could be harmful to people and wildlife. Assessors might work with consulting companies to write risk assessments or prepare technical presentations for organizations concerned about the environmental safety of a particular site.

Environmental site assessors travel from site to site to perform field investigations. Their responsibilities can include analytical materials analysis, designing specifications for cleaning up a hazardous site, and environmental assessments.

Environmental site assessors follow guidelines outlined by the American Society for Testing and Materials (ASTM; www.astm.org) and send completed reports to property owners, lawyers, lenders, and other interested parties.

A bachelor's degree in environmental or natural science is the minimum requirement for an entry-level environmental site assessor. A master's degree is preferred, however. ASTM offers additional training and certification in several categories, including property condition assessments, environmental regulatory compliance audits, and risk-based corrective action applied at petroleum release sites.

Environmental site assessors can work for governmental agencies, consulting firms, and industrial companies.

The growing population has put increased demands on the environment, making opportunities for environmental site assessors plentiful, according to the U.S. Bureau of Labor Statistics (BLS). Job prospects are particularly good for environmental site assessors who specialize in *hydrology*, the fastest growing sector within the environmental sector.

The average annual salary for an environmental site assessor is $56,170.

def•i•ni•tion

Hydrology is a science dealing with the properties, distribution, and circulation of water.

Brownfield Redevelopment Specialist

Brownfield redevelopment specialists provide comprehensive assessments on the cleanup and possible reuse of *brownfield sites*. They travel to various sites, performing site assessments, consulting on possible development scenarios, evaluating the environmental costs and benefits of redevelopment, examining tax incentives, and preparing plans. In the course of their work, brownfield redevelopment specialists may collaborate with federal, state, and local governments; landowners; real estate brokers; developers; urban planners; environmental assessment firms; and the public.

def•i•ni•tion

Brownfield sites are often former industrial settings that are currently abandoned, vacant, or underutilized because of the presence or potential presence of hazardous substances, pollutants, or contaminants. Common brownfield sites include former gas stations, dry cleaners, factories, and closed military bases.

The minimum requirement for a brownfield redevelopment specialist is a bachelor's degree in urban planning, environmental science, or a related field. A master's degree is preferred, though.

The U.S. Environmental Protection Agency (EPA) (www.epa.gov) offers a Brownfields Job Training Program that provides training to help those who live near brownfield sites train for jobs as skilled environmental technicians to assist with brownfield redevelopment. To date, more than 4,000 trainees have graduated from the program.

Brownfield redevelopment specialists earn an average annual salary of $33,000.

> **Inside Scoop**
>
> Funds from the EPA Brownfields Program have resulted in $6.5 billion in cleanup and development of brownfield sites, creating more than 25,000 jobs in the public and private sectors.

Conservation Engineer

Conservation engineers are responsible for the design and implementation of conservation practices. In the course of their work, conservation engineers might conduct engineering surveys, develop designs and cost estimates for conservation practices, review erosion control and waste management plans, and review construction site erosion control plans. Their work is often done on behalf of local, state, and federal governments and landowners.

Conservation engineers may choose to specialize in water conservation or soil conservation.

Private consulting firms and government agencies are the major employers of conservation engineers.

To work as a conservation engineer, a candidate should have a bachelor's degree with a major in environmental or civil engineering, resource management, hydrology, geology, or another related field.

On average, conservation engineers earn $55,000 per year.

Design and Development

The success of a green building starts with its design. Before the foundation is poured and the first boards are nailed into place, professionals such as architects, *LEED* consultants, and interior designers work together to design buildings that are sustainable and beautiful. To this end, the National Association of Home Builders (www.nahb.org) developed the National Green Building Program (www.nahbgreen.org) to help design and development professionals in the building industry go green. New certifications and job categories have led to expanded job opportunities in the design and development of green buildings.

def•i•ni•tion

LEED is an acronym for Leadership in Energy and Environmental Design, a voluntary, consensus-based national standard enacted by the U.S. Green Building Council for the design, construction, and operation of high-performance, sustainable buildings.

Architect

Architects design buildings, turning their ideas into images and plans. A career in architecture is about more than just design; architects are involved in all aspects of a construction project, from site selection to overseeing final inspections. Their responsibilities can include conducting feasibility and environmental impact studies, preparing cost analysis studies, examining land use regulations, and developing comprehensive plans for client review.

After plans are approved, architects develop comprehensive construction plans. Their blueprints include drawings of the structural systems; air-conditioning, heating, ventilation, and electrical systems; and plumbing. Plans also provide specifics of the building materials to be used for the project.

During the development of a design, architects take into account things such as building codes, zoning laws, and other ordinances.

Although architects are trained to design a wide range of structures, including houses, schools, hospitals, churches, factories, office buildings, college campuses, and industrial parks, some choose to specialize. Areas of specialization range from designing certain types of buildings, such as airport terminals or skyscrapers, to planning and predesign consultations for construction management.

Knowledge of software such as Computer-Aided Design and Drafting (CADD) and Building Information Modeling (BIM) is essential for creating design and construction drawings.

The demand for buildings that incorporate recycled and sustainable materials, are designed for maximum energy efficiency, and reduce pollution and land development impacts has created new opportunities for architects.

Architects who understand the principles of green building and can incorporate it into their designs, especially those who are familiar with the LEED Rating System, have the best employment prospects.

Currently, only 10,000 *LEED APs* work in architecture in the United States. Earning certification as a LEED AP can provide better opportunities for architects who want to work in the green building industry.

Inside Scoop
The American Institute of Architects (www.aia.org) has initiated a strategy called Sustainability 2030 that aims for the design of all buildings by the year 2030 to be carbon neutral.

def•i•ni•tion

LEED AP stands for Leadership in Energy and Environmental Design Accredited Professional. A LEED AP is certified through the Green Building Certification Institute (www.gbci.org) as a professional who has demonstrated a thorough understanding of green building practices and principles and the LEED rating system. Since the professional accreditation program was launched in 2001, more than 43,000 people have earned the credential.

All states require architects to be licensed. Licensing requirements include a bachelor's degree in architecture, an internship, a passing score on all divisions of the Architect Registration Examination, and at least three years of practical work training. Earning a master's degree in architecture can boost employment options. Each state sets its own guidelines to enable architects to complete all the eligibility requirements.

During the time between graduation and licensure, graduates often work in the field under the supervision of a licensed architect.

Most states also require some form of continuing education to maintain a license, ranging from self-study courses, conferences, workshops, to college classes.

There are 132,000 licensed architects in the United States. Nearly 70 percent of architects work in architectural and engineering firms, according to the BLS. Architects can, however, also work for residential construction firms or government agencies. Approximately 1 in 5 architects is self-employed.

Career Crisis

The BLS notes that architects who are seeking work as office and retail space designers are facing strong competition for employment as a result of the struggling economy. Major changes in the housing market have had limited impact on job opportunities for architects because residential construction makes up such a small portion of work for architects. Architects who design schools, hospitals, correctional facilities, and other institutional buildings are less affected by fluctuations in the economy.

Architects earn an average annual income of $64,150.

LEED Consultant

LEED consultant is one of the newest jobs created by the green building industry. A LEED consultant's role is to coordinate all aspects of the LEED certification process for a building project, from researching LEED criteria to preparing the appropriate paperwork for submittal. In addition to consulting on various approaches to earning certification, LEED consultants also provide information on the latest policies and regulations relating to LEED certification.

On a day-to-day basis, LEED consultants might perform LEED rating analyses and create and deliver presentations on LEED certification.

Most LEED consultants are LEED APs with bachelor's degrees in architecture or engineering, and have extensive experience in construction and trades. Project management experience, especially on LEED-certified buildings, is helpful.

> **Inside Scoop**
>
> Earning LEED certification is an extensive process that requires multiple steps. The U.S. Green Building Council (www.usgbc.org) provides detailed information about all aspects of LEED certification on its website.

LEED consultants number 1,200 in the United States—an increase of 111 percent since 2005.

The average annual salary for a LEED consultant is $86,000.

Sustainability Analyst

Sustainability analysts, also called green building analysts, consult on the overall sustainability of a building, not just the elements that lead to LEED certification.

Sustainability analysts work alongside architects and engineers to integrate green features into building design. They consult on site selection, assist with the development of strategic plans to make new and existing buildings more environmentally friendly, and provide research on emerging green technologies. Their duties can also include researching and writing technical reports on the cost-benefit analysis of green design and available tax incentives.

A bachelor's degree in science, engineering, or technical management is required to secure a position as a sustainability analyst. A master's degree or Ph.D., along with a background in architecture or engineering and extensive experience in the green building industry, is preferred.

Sustainability analysts can expect to earn $66,530 on average per year.

Interior Designer

Interior designers enhance the function and aesthetics of interior spaces by implementing principles of good design. An interior designer meets with her client to determine his needs, taking into account his budget and personal aesthetics. After gathering basic information, the interior designer develops a design plan that includes detailed sketches and a proposed budget.

After the plans are approved, the interior designer develops a timeline for the project, hires contractors and coordinates their work schedules, oversees the installation of the design, and addresses client questions.

During a project, interior designers might work with architects to address any structural concerns, and work with construction inspectors to ensure the design meets building codes.

In addition to incorporating basics such as color and texture, interior designers often incorporate environmentally friendly design elements, including recycled and sustainable materials, chemical-free and hypoallergenic fabrics and finishes, energy-efficient lighting, and low *VOC* paints.

def•i•ni•tion

VOCs are volatile organic compounds, the chemicals found in paints and stains that release harmful pollutants into the atmosphere.

Green Guidance

The American Society of Interior Designers (ASID) is the largest professional association for interior designers in the United States.

The demand for green design led the U.S. Green Building Council and the *American Society of Interior Designers (ASID)* (www.asid.org) to develop REGREEN (www.regreenprogram.org) in 2008. REGREEN is a set of guidelines for designing sustainable interiors. The program was designed to increase understanding of green design, provide information on environmentally friendly materials, and outline the benefits of sustainable design to homeowners, interior designers, and service providers.

ASID has also developed a set of guiding principles for environmental stewardship among its members. The principles include advocating for the use of environmentally friendly products and the reduction of energy use.

An interior designer with a bachelor's degree has the best job prospects. A total of 23 states, including the District of Columbia and Puerto Rico, register or license interior designers. The National Kitchen & Bath Association (www.nkba.org) offers additional certifications, including several in green design.

Membership in a professional association such as ASID is a measure of an interior designer's qualifications and professional standing. An interior designer with at least a two-year degree and work experience can qualify for membership in ASID.

Interior designers can also seek certification as LEED APs. Currently, the United States has 1,200 LEED APs in interior design.

Approximately 26 percent of interior designers are self-employed, according to the BLS.

The average annual salary for an interior designer is $42,260.

Residential and Commercial Construction

Construction is one of the fastest-growing segments of the green building industry. According to the American Institute of Architects, one in five cities with populations of 500,000 or more has a green building program—a 418 percent since 2003. The number of green buildings in the United States has topped 60 million, according to the Green Building Resource Center, and an estimated 38 million additional green buildings will be constructed by 2010. The impact is undeniable: Green buildings conserve natural resources, improve air quality, reduce waste, and minimize energy consumption. The impact on employment is just as strong. The skyrocketing demand for green buildings has created an abundance of new job opportunities in the building sector.

General Contractor

Every construction site, whether residential, commercial, or industrial, has a general contractor. A general contractor coordinates all aspects of a construction project, from creating a timeline to hiring the subcontractors.

The growth of the green building industry has made it increasingly important for general contractors to be able to provide direction and oversight for LEED projects. In fact, the general contractor is responsible for at least 18 of the 69 credits of the LEED rating system. During the construction process, the general contractor works closely with the architect, consulting engineers, construction manager, and (possibly) a LEED-accredited professional to ensure all the elements are in place to earn the LEED credits necessary for certification.

During the initial planning phases, a general contractor is made aware of each LEED credit being attempted and must monitor progress throughout construction to ensure the credits are achieved. It's essential for a general contractor to understand the rationale behind materials specifications on a LEED project because even a small deviation can jeopardize the LEED credit.

Licensing requirements for contractors vary from state to state. Certain states, including Oregon, Nevada, and Tennessee, require contractors to be state licensed. In North Carolina, only contractors working on projects costing more than $30,000 must be licensed, and in Nebraska, licenses are required only for general contractors working in counties with populations of 100,000 or more.

Some general contractors hold bachelor's degrees in construction science, building science, civil engineering, or construction management; others are former construction workers who have progressed through the ranks to become general contractors.

Green Advantage (www.greenadvantage.org) offers a specialized program—the Green Advantage Builders Certification—that enables contractors to certify their knowledge of green building.

Although the U.S. Census Bureau reports that construction of office space, commercial buildings, and lodging continues to decline, the employment outlook for general contractors remains strong. Manufacturing construction has increased 27.4 percent since 2007, according to the BLS, employment for general contractors is expected to increase by 10 percent by 2016, due in large part to the number of general contractors expected to retire in the next decade.

There are 487,000 licensed general contractors in the United States, and almost 1,500 of them are LEED APs; about 57 percent are self-employed, many as owners of construction firms.

The median income for a licensed general contractor is $73,700.

Construction Manager

Construction managers oversee the overall construction project. Their duties include project and cost management, ensuring on-the-job safety, communicating with subcontractors, and resolving disputes on the job site. Construction managers generally report to general contractors.

The construction manager might have a main office or a field office, but most construction managers work on the job site of a specific project. Extensive travel can be required if the construction site is not located near the main office.

Most construction managers are on call 24 hours per day. They can be called on to deal with emergencies on job sites, delayed materials shipments, and the effects of bad weather. The typical workweek is often longer than 40 hours because of construction deadlines.

Experienced construction workers can work their way up to construction management positions. Some employers want to hire construction managers with bachelor's degrees in construction management or civil engineering. Associations such as the American Council for Construction Education (www.acce-hq.org) and the Associated Schools of Construction (www.ascweb.org) also provide certification programs for construction managers.

The construction manager overseeing construction of a LEED-certified building must be familiar with the compliance requirements and will be responsible for overseeing the day-to-day implementation of LEED standards.

Because the LEED rating system for new construction has been in place only since 2000, construction managers have to closely supervise subcontractors and suppliers to ensure they're on target to meet LEED standards.

Achieving LEED certification requires significant documentation. The construction manager is responsible for ensuring that the documentation is completed and filed in a timely manner.

According to the BLS, construction managers hold 487,000 jobs. Currently, more than 1,800 LEED APs work in construction management in the United States.

The average salary for a construction manager is $69,400 per year.

> **Inside Scoop**
>
> The stringent requirements to achieve LEED certification have made the construction process more complex. To this end, employers are placing more importance on hiring general contractors with specialized education.

Building Inspector

Building inspectors are responsible for assessing residential and commercial buildings to ensure they comply with building codes and ordinances, zoning regulations, and contract specifications. They might inspect new construction, remodels, or repairs/retrofits.

It's essential for a building inspector who is assessing a green building to be familiar with the latest technologies relating to energy efficiency and sustainable materials.

Many states require building inspectors to be licensed; licensing requirements vary from state to state. A high school diploma or GED is required, and post-secondary education in engineering or architecture is desirable.

The demand for building inspectors who can assess the sustainable attributes of products led the International Code Council (www.iccsafe.org) to develop a certification program called Sustainable Attribute Verification Evaluation (SAVE). The first classes were offered in 2008.

Currently, 110,000 licensed building inspectors are working in the United States, and just 20 of those are LEED APs in codes and inspections. Employment opportunities for building inspectors are expected to grow by 18 percent by 2016.

The average salary for a building inspector is $46,570.

Electrician

The demand for energy-efficient lighting has created job opportunities for electricians. Electricians are responsible for bringing electricity into homes and businesses. They install and maintain the wiring, fuses, and other electrical components. Green electricians have up-to-date knowledge on energy-efficient lighting, heating, and air conditioning; can advise on the payback periods for energy-efficient appliances; and are familiar with emerging technologies like *LEDs* and *CFLs*.

def•i•ni•tion

An **LED** is a light-emitting diode. LEDs are often used in traffic signals, cameras, and telephone dials. They produce more light per watt than incandescent bulbs, making them an energy-efficient choice.

A **CFL** is a compact fluorescent lightbulb. CFLs use 75 percent less energy than standard incandescent bulbs and last up to 10 times longer.

Electricians can also offer suggestions for improving the energy efficiency of the electrical systems for residential, commercial, or industrial use.

Electricians often complete an apprenticeship program lasting up to five years. In most states, electricians are required to be licensed. There are 705,000 licensed electricians in the United States, according to the BLS.

The average hourly wage for an electrician is $20.97.

Carpenter

Carpenters build, install, and repair structures made from wood. The types of jobs carpenters perform vary widely from constructing bridges to building decks. On the job, carpenters must be able to read blueprints, measure and mark building materials, cut and shape materials such as wood and fiberglass, use nails and screws to join various pieces, and check the accuracy of their work.

Green carpenters might specialize in using sustainable woods, products certified by the *Forest Stewardship Council (FSC)*, recycled and salvaged building materials, low VOC stains, and water-based wood finishes—all of which can help earn credits toward LEED certification.

Depending on the project, carpenters might work onsite (indoors or outdoors) or in a workshop. Approximately 32 percent of carpenters are self-employed.

The job requires standing for long periods of time, bending, climbing, and kneeling. Carpenters should be physically fit, have good hand-eye coordination, and be comfortable working with power tools.

Green Guidance

Forest Stewardship Council (FSC) wood comes from certified well-managed forests. The FSC standards have been applied in 57 countries around the world. Visit the FSC website at www.fscus.org to find out more.

Carpenters learn their trade through a combination of on-the-job training and apprenticeship programs. Carpenters make up the largest building trades occupation. More than 1.5 million carpenters are employed in the United States.

The average hourly rate for a carpenter is $17.57.

Materials and System Performance

More than three billion tons of raw materials are used in construction projects on an annual basis worldwide. Choosing green building materials promotes the conservation of dwindling nonrenewable resources. Optimizing their performance helps reduce environmental impact by improving energy efficiency, enhancing indoor air quality, and conserving water; this makes materials and system performance an integral component of green building.

Energy Auditor

Energy auditors work with residential and commercial customers to review their energy usage and make recommendations for increased energy efficiency. Their job includes communicating the benefits of energy-saving measures to clients and providing information about available financial incentive programs and energy-efficient mortgages, when applicable.

During an energy audit, the auditor checks filters, hot water heater settings, thermostat usage, vent leakage, insulation, pool controls, and other energy systems in the building. An energy audit is conducted using equipment such as *blower doors* and *infrared cameras*. After the audit is complete, the energy auditor prepares a comprehensive report detailing changes that will result in increased energy efficiency. The recommendations can range from upgrading to CFLs to replacing entire ventilation systems.

def•i•ni•tion

Blower doors are powerful fans that mount on an exterior door and measure the amount of air loss in a building.

Infrared cameras are used to reveal hard-to-detect areas of air infiltration.

Energy auditors can work for private businesses or government agencies such as local utility companies. For most positions, a minimum of a bachelor's degree is required. It's also helpful to have a background in construction or heating, ventilation, and air conditioning (HVAC).

The Residential Energy Services Network (www. resnet.us) offers a Home Energy Rater certification that allows energy auditors to certify building energy performance for federal tax credit qualification and EPA ENERGY STAR–labeled homes.

Energy auditors can also seek verifier certification through Built Green (www. builtgreen.net). The third-party certification is an optional credit, initiated by the builder, to achieve Built Green Certification. Upon completion of the program, residential technical specialists are able to assess residential and commercial construction sites for their environmental impacts.

The Association of Energy Engineers (www.aeecenter.org) also offers training to become a Certified Energy Auditor (CEA) and Certified Energy Auditor in Training (CEAIT). The programs are currently offered only outside the United States, but certifications are recognized by U.S. companies.

The demand for increased energy efficiency has led to increased opportunities for energy auditors. In fact, the BLS labeled energy auditor as one of the new and emerging occupations in the green economy.

Energy auditors can expect to earn upwards of $42,000 annually.

Green Materials Expert

Green materials experts promote the use of building materials that have minimal impact on the environment. Their role is to help clients such as interior designers, architects, and builders select materials that are natural, chemical-free, energy efficient, and locally manufactured.

Green materials experts can play a role in a building earning LEED certification. According to U.S. Green Building Council (USGBC) guidelines, material selection is its own category, accounting for 13 points toward LEED certification.

After an initial planning meeting with clients, a green materials expert prepares detailed plans highlighting options for environmentally friendly materials. Her job is to recommend materials that fit with the aesthetic and budget of the project.

A bachelor's degree, coupled with a background in architecture, interior design, or engineering, is helpful for pursuing work as a green materials expert. Knowledge of LEED standards is essential.

The National Sustainable Building Advisor (www.nasbap.org) program also offers a nine-month program leading to accreditation as a Certified Sustainable Building Advisor.

Green materials experts typically work for architecture and planning firms, engineering companies, construction contractors, government agencies, and interior design firms.

The median salary for a green materials expert is $64,220 per year.

Eco-Friendly Landscaping

The trees, plants, soil, and water in our landscape contribute to the overall health and beauty of our environment. Environmentally friendly landscape design and maintenance has significant benefits, including conserving water, reducing stormwater runoff, creating additional wildlife habitats, reducing energy use, and protecting existing natural areas.

Eco-friendly landscaping is appropriate for settings ranging from parks, to highway right-of-ways, to industrial complexes, to private homes.

Workers in these fields can have significant impacts on the planet, especially when they use nontoxic pesticides and herbicides, employ water-saving strategies, and promote the growth of native plants.

Landscape Architect

Landscape architects create designs for outdoor spaces such as residential neighborhoods, public parks, shopping centers, college campuses, and golf courses. A landscape architect's goal is to create designs that are functional, beautiful, and compatible with the natural environment.

After analyzing natural elements of a site, such as climate, soil condition, drainage, and existing vegetation, a landscape architect creates detailed plans of the site. His plans include sketches, models, photographs, and cost estimates as well as detailed information about material selection. Some use video simulation and computer-mapping systems to create landscape plans for clients. Their designs take into account land use regulations, including protecting wetlands and historic resources. After a design is approved, the landscape architect oversees site construction and installation of plantings.

Landscape architects can help earn credits toward LEED certification. Landscapes that feature environmentally friendly elements like native plants and highly efficient irrigation systems can account for up to 27 credits—up to 40 percent of the total credits needed to earn LEED certification.

Some landscape architects work on a variety of projects, whereas others opt to specialize in one specific area such as parks, highway beautification, waterfront improvement, or residential design.

Landscape architects might also work in environmental remediation; designing and planning the restoration of natural spaces like wetlands, stream corridors, mined areas, and forested land; and abatement of stormwater run-off in new developments. During the course of their work, landscape architects might collaborate with scientists, foresters, and other environmental professionals to assess the best ways to conserve or restore natural resources.

Landscape architects might also be called on to prepare environmental impact statements and studies on environmental issues such as public land-use planning.

Organizations ranging from real estate development firms and government agencies to garden centers and individual homeowners employ landscape architects.

Career Crisis

The current downturn in new construction has led to greater competition for jobs among landscape architects and has resulted in layoffs for those employed by builders. Because landscape architects can work on a variety of projects across a number of fields, including parks and recreation, historic preservation, and wetland rehabilitation, the BLS still expects employment opportunities to increase by 16 percent by 2016.

Landscape architects require a minimum of an undergraduate degree, either a bachelor of landscape architecture or a bachelor of science in landscape architecture. Some positions require a master's degree in landscape architecture.

According to the American Society of Landscape Architects (www.asla.org), 49 states require landscape architects to be licensed. Vermont is the only state that doesn't require licensure.

To become licensed, landscape architects must complete the Landscape Architect Registration Examination (LARE) sponsored by the Council of Landscape Architectural Registration Boards (www.clarb.org). Prior to taking the exam, landscape architects must earn a degree in an accredited program and have at least one year of work experience. In states where licensure is required, new graduates are often called *apprentices* or *intern landscape architects* until they become licensed.

Green Guidance

Because licensing requirements vary from state to state, it can be difficult for landscape architects to transfer their registrations from one state to another. Meeting national standards by obtaining certification from the Council of Landscape Architectural Registration Boards can be useful for obtaining reciprocal licensure in other states.

To maintain a license, most states require landscape architects to participate in some form of continuing education. The requirements vary from state to state, but often include the completion of workshops, seminars, classes, or attendance at conferences.

Landscape architects can also earn certification as LEED APs. Currently, 707 LEED APs work in landscape architecture. Earning certification can improve employment prospects for landscape architects.

More than 50 percent of landscape architects work for architectural or engineering firms; 6 percent work for governmental agencies; and almost 20 percent are self-employed.

On average, landscape architects earn $57,980 per year.

Horticulturalist

Horticulturists are experts in the science of plant cultivation. Their job is to devise the best methods for breeding, propagating, and growing plants to improve crop yield and resistance to insects and diseases, boost nutritional value, and reduce environmental stresses. They can specialize in several areas including propagation and cultivation, plant biochemistry and physiology, breeding and genetic engineering, and crop production.

The demand for conservation and restoration projects has stimulated growth in the industry, creating new jobs. A growing number of horticulturalists are specializing in environmental horticulture, an area of study that includes restoring natural areas, moderating climactic conditions, and using native plants.

Horticulturalists can work in a wide range of organizations such as nurseries/greenhouses, government or educational institutions, and private botanical gardens. Their job titles can include cropping systems engineers, propagators, crop inspectors, extension specialists, plant breeders, research scientists, and crop production advisors.

A minimum of a bachelor's degree is required to work as a horticulturalist. In some fields, horticulturalists need a master's degree or a Ph.D. in horticultural science.

The average annual salary for a horticulturalist is $52,052.

Green Roof Designer

Green roof designers create the designs and choose the materials for *green roofs*.

def•i•ni•tion

> **Green roofs,** also known as living roofs, are rooftop gardens filled with plants such as sedum, wildflowers, and native grasses. They are installed on the rooftops of homes, high rises, office buildings, schools, and hospitals around the world. Green roofs reduce air pollution and stormwater runoff, mitigate noise, and act as wildlife habitats.

During the planning phase, a green roof designer measures the size, slope, and height of the roof; assesses drainage elements like drains and buried conduits; and examines other rooftop systems including solar panels. The green roof designer also meets with clients to discuss the budget, intended use of the green roof, and their aesthetic preferences before coming up with a design.

Green roof designers often collaborate with landscape architects and structural engineers to ensure their designs are appropriate for their projects. A typical green roof design incorporate systems for drainage, plant nourishment, protection of underlying waterproofing systems, and ongoing maintenance.

Inside Scoop

National Research Council Canada (www.nrc-cnrc.gc.ca) found that a green roof on a building less than three stories high could reduce the average daily cooling demands by 50 percent—compared to a typical flat roof—and can reduce stormwater runoff by up to 95 percent, lowering the impact on municipal storm drainage systems.

A green roof can earn credits toward LEED certification. Specifically, green roof designers can help earn credits for stormwater design, water efficiency, energy performance, and regional materials.

The International Code Council (www.iccsafe.org) regulates standards for green roof design and installation; green roof designers must adhere to the code requirements when designing green roofs. The National Roofing Contractors Association (www.nrca.net) and the American Standard Testing Methods (www.astm.org) are in the process of developing guidelines for designing and testing procedures for green roofs.

Green roof designers often have bachelor's degrees in landscape architecture or engineering. Green Roofs for Healthy Cities (www.greenroofs.org) is in the process of developing certification to become a Green Roof Professional (GRP). The expected launch date for the program is spring 2009. Currently, the organization offers classes such as "Green Roof Infrastructure: Design and Implementation" and "Green Roof Infrastructure: Waterproofing and Drainage" in cities across North America.

Due to the newness of the profession, statistics on the average salaries for green roof designers are difficult to pin down. According to Green Roofs for Healthy Cities, green roof designers in established firms can expect to earn salaries comparable to landscape architects and civil engineers.

Arborist

Arborists are tree doctors who diagnose diseases, nutrient deficiencies, and structural problems with trees and shrubs. A typical day on the job can include identifying bacteria, fungus, or insect infestation in a tree; pruning dead or diseased tree limbs; and offering advice on disease control, watering, and fertilization. Arborists might assist landscape designers in choosing trees and shrubs.

Arborists can have significant impacts on the environment by using nontoxic chemicals to treat diseases and pests, using green fertilizers, pruning to promote healthy growth, and suggesting native plant species for landscape plans. To protect trees, arborists can use minimally invasive techniques, such as using ropes to climb trees instead of using spurs attached to their boots, which leave small holes in the trunks.

Approximately 12,000 certified arborists are working in the United States, although certification is not required. Thousands more arborists are working without certification. Some have high school diplomas and learned their skills on the job; others have advanced education in subjects such as forestry and horticulture.

Arborists can seek certification through the International Society of Arboriculture (www.isa-arbor.com) or the Tree Care Industry Association (www.tcia.org).

Arborists might work for tree care companies or for state and local governments, taking care of trees on public property such as parks and roadsides. Some arborists are self-employed.

The average hourly wage for an arborist is $9.50 an hour.

Green Roof Installer

Green roof installers put waterproof membranes on rooftops, add layers of soil, plant vegetation, and install irrigation systems. The demand for their skills is growing rapidly.

The installation of a green roof helps earn credits toward LEED certification, making green roof installers major players in the greening of schools, libraries, college campuses, government offices, high rises, and homes.

It is much more labor-intensive to install a green roof than a regular roof, but laborers require many of the same skills: the ability to lift up to 50 pounds, climb ladders, and balance on rooftops. The work is performed outdoors and requires traveling to job sites, so installers might need a driver's license. Roofing and landscaping experience are bonuses.

> **Inside Scoop**
>
> In the United States, the demand for green roofs increased up to 61 percent in 2007, creating new jobs for installers.

Green roof installation is a relatively new occupation in the United States, so most companies offer training programs and allow installers to perfect their skills on the job site. Green Roofs for Healthy Cities also offers classes for installers.

Careers in green roof installation are so new that it's difficult to find statistics on salaries, though most can expect to earn approximately $15.51 per hour—the average salary earned by a conventional roofer.

Nursery Worker

Nursery workers, also called greenhouse workers, take care of trees, shrubs, and flowers. Their jobs can include propagating seeds, transplanting, watering, pruning, fertilizing, and harvesting. Nursery workers might also be responsible for cutting sod, loading plants onto trucks to fill orders, and performing customer service duties.

A growing number of nurseries are incorporating green practices into their operations. Nursery workers are often on the frontlines of these programs, participating directly in efforts to propagate native plants from cuttings, using efficient irrigation systems, recycling plant pots, and composting green waste. Nursery workers in customer service roles can talk to shoppers about the benefits of native plants; direct them to nontoxic fertilizers, pesticides, and herbicides; and recommend eco-friendly garden furniture and accessories.

Most nursery workers are employed by greenhouses and garden centers. The work is often seasonal and can require long hours and weekend work from March to September—the height of the growing season.

Working conditions vary dramatically, although it is almost always physically demanding and, because most of the work is performed outdoors, requires working in extreme temperatures.

Certificates in greenhouse gardening are available through community colleges, but most nursery workers learn their skills through on-the-job training. A bachelor's degree in horticulture, soil science, or greenhouse management might be required to advance to nursery/greenhouse manager. The ability to speak both English and Spanish is also helpful for those who seek supervisory roles.

Green Guidance

The American Nursery and Landscape Association offers educational programs and networking opportunities to members. Visit www.anla.org to find out more.

Most states also have greenhouse associations. Go to www.startanursery.com/associations.php for a state-by-state listing.

The average wage for a nursery worker is $7.95 an hour.

Chapter 4

Renewable Energy

In This Chapter

- ◆ Careers in the research, development, sales, transportation, and installation of renewable energy and related products

- ◆ Opportunities for everyone from high school graduates to those with Ph.D.s

- ◆ Legislation that could impact job growth in the wind energy industry

- ◆ Job growth in the bioenergy industry that is fueled by consumer demand

- ◆ Certifications to help solar installers outshine the competition

The development of renewable sources of energy has emerged as one of the main solutions to global warming. Unlike coal, natural gas, and oil, which are significant sources of pollution, renewable energy sources like solar power and geothermal energy have almost no environmental impact. Harnessing the power of the sun, wind, water, and heat for power is not just good for the environment, but is also good for the economy.

A report issued by the Environmental Law & Policy Center (www.elpc. org) titled *Putting Renewables to Work: How Many Jobs Can the Clean Energy Industry Generate?* states that the renewable energy industry has consistently generated more jobs per megawatt of electricity than the fossil fuel industry has generated. In fact, the American Solar Energy Society (www.ases.org) estimates that the renewable energy industry could create 40 million jobs by 2030 in the United States alone.

Careers in the renewable energy industry are as varied as the sources of green power. Some require a high school diploma and on-the-job training, whereas others require a graduate degree and significant industry experience. Whether the job entails welding the metal frames for solar panels or researching new renewable energy technologies, the outcome is the same: great careers in green power.

Wind Power

The idea of using wind to generate power is not new, but the technologies used to improve the effectiveness of wind power are under continual development, leading to a glut of new jobs. Wind power has become one of the fastest-growing sources of renewable energy, with wind farms popping up in almost every state across the country. According to the American Solar Energy Society, wind power was directly or indirectly responsible for the creation of 53,000 jobs in 2006. Over the past six years, wind-generation capacity has increased more than 400 percent and is expected to grow an additional 21 percent per year, to a value of more than $80 billion by 2016.

Wind Energy Engineer

Wind energy engineers manage all aspects of wind power projects from site selection through the final inspections of *wind turbines*. The job entails conceptualizing, developing, and evaluating new methods to enhance the mechanics, hydraulics, and software performance of wind turbines; designing the layout of *wind farms* to account for access roads, land boundaries, and environmental studies; and applying for environmental permits to comply with local, state, and federal requirements.

Wind energy engineers also provide technical support for turbine and generator design, manage sediment and erosion control plans, and direct the review of wind farm electrical design. They might specialize in a specific aspect of wind energy, such as utility scale wind farms, community wind systems, or offshore wind projects.

def•i•ni•tion

Wind turbines are rotating machines that generate mechanical power. The mechanical power can be channeled through a generator and converted into electricity. The United States generates more wind power than any other nation in the world, with total installed wind power capacity in excess of 19,549 megawatts.

Wind farms are plots of land with several wind turbines that are used for the production of electric power. The states with the highest number of wind farms are Texas, California, and Iowa, according to the American Wind Energy Association (www. awea.org).

Wind energy engineers work for power plants, engineering firms, construction companies, nonprofit organizations, and utilities.

Career Crisis

The expiration of the federal production tax credit at the end of 2008 is threatening the growth of the wind power industry. Over the past 18 months, at least 41 facilities have been announced, opened, or expanded in the United States. The American Wind Energy Association worries that, without a renewal of the tax credit, advances in the industry—as well as job growth—will stall.

A bachelor's degree in civil engineering is essential, and a growing number of positions require a master's degree.

The American Wind Energy Association and the United States Energy Association (www.usea.org) offer job listings and up-to-date information on the latest projects, advances in technology, and policy developments in the field of wind energy. Several states also have regional associations, such as the Iowa Wind Energy Association (www.iowawindenergy.org) and the California Wind Energy Association (www.calwea. org), that provide resources to regional members.

The median wage for a wind energy engineer is $71,710 per year.

Wind Resource Analyst

Wind resource analysts review meteorological data and make recommendations for the design, development, and implementation of wind energy products. Their duties include identifying site topography and wind resources, analyzing data from meteoro-logical towers and wind maps, estimating energy production and losses based on wind turbine options, designing wind farm layouts to maximize energy output, preparing wind assessments using software such as WindFarmer, and developing photo simulations of potential projects.

Wind resource analysts are often involved during the planning stages of a project to ensure wind farms are designed for optimal energy production and maximum profitability. Sometimes, they are called in to evaluate an existing project to recommend alterations and enhancements to products and procedures.

Inside Scoop

There is evidence that global warming alters wind patterns, which affects the location of future wind farms and might reduce the effectiveness of existing wind turbines. Wind resource analysts review this data and make recommendations about minimizing the effects of global warming on wind power generation.

To analyze meteorological data, wind resource analysts need to be proficient in programming languages such as Fortran, BASIC, Unix/Linux, S-Plus, and C++, as well as mapping tools like Global Mapper.

Wind resource analysts need at least a minimum of a bachelor's degree in meteorology, atmospheric science, engineering, or physics. Most positions require a master's degree or Ph.D. in climatology, meteorology, or engineering.

The median salary for a wind resource analyst is $77,150 per year.

Electrical Engineer

Electrical engineers design, develop, and test electrical equipment for navigation systems, electrical utilities, power generation, and transmission devices. Electrical engineers often focus on the generation and supply of power, including renewable energy.

Electrical engineers play an important role in the development of wind energy. In this field, their jobs can include testing turbine generator installations, overseeing the installation and testing of underground and overhead power lines, maintaining turbine equipment, and collecting data on turbine performance for analysis.

Electrical engineers are responsible for reviewing utility interconnection requirements to ensure compliance, preparing formal specifications for electrical components that are outsourced, and investigating and resolving electrical problems identified during turbine installation and commissioning. They might also prepare plans, schematics, and material lists for wind energy projects; provide cost estimates; and develop construction specifications.

There are 153,000 electrical engineers in the United States, and the majority work for manufacturing companies and engineering firms. Opportunities for electrical engineers are expected to grow 6 percent by 2016. The U.S. Bureau of Labor Statistics (BLS) predicts that the greatest demand will be in the fields of power generation and telecommunications.

> ### Inside Scoop
>
> The Global Wind Energy Council (www.gwec.net) reports that the total value of power-generating equipment installed around the world last year was more than $14 billion—and electrical engineers are involved in various aspects of its design, installation, and testing.

The job requires a bachelor's degree in electrical engineering or a related field; a master's degree or Ph.D. improves employment options.

The Institute of Electrical and Electronics Engineers, Inc. (www.ieee.org) offers continuing education classes, conferences, industry news, and job listings to members.

Electrical engineers earn a median salary of $75,930 per year.

Wind Turbine Technician

Wind turbine technicians perform inspections and repairs on the electrical and mechanical systems and control equipment used to run wind turbines. Their responsibilities include inspecting, troubleshooting, calibrating, cleaning, maintaining, and repairing the various systems to ensure optimal performance. Specifically, wind turbine technicians conduct vibration analyses, execute diagnostic tests, perform scheduled maintenance, and maintain accurate records on all service and repair work. They must be comfortable working with tools like multimeters, amp clamps, and torque tools; reading complex diagrams, prints, and schematics; and lifting up to 45 pounds.

> ### Inside Scoop
>
> A modern 600kW wind turbine recovers all the energy used over its life cycle, from manufacturing to its eventual removal, within the first three months of being put into use, according to a study by the Danish Wind Turbine Manufacturers Association (www.windpower.org/en/core.htm). This makes wind power one of the most eco-friendly forms of energy at all stages of development and implementation.

Wind turbine technicians can be exposed to extreme heat or cold because the bulk of their work is performed outdoors. The job also requires working at heights, often on platforms that are more than 250 feet in the air.

Wind turbine technicians need a high school diploma or a GED.

To meet the growing demand for qualified candidates, several colleges have begun offering certificates to turbine technicians. The Laramie County Community College (www.lccc.cc.wy.us) in Wyoming offers three programs: basic wind technician, intermediate wind technician, and associate of science in wind energy; Riverland Community College (www.riverland.edu) in Minnesota offers a wind turbine technician-renewable energy diploma; and Iowa Lakes Community College (www.iowalakes.edu) has a program in turbine technology and renewable energy.

Wind turbine technicians earn a median wage of $18 per hour.

Millwright

Millwrights install, replace, and repair machines and other equipment that are used to generate power, including wind power, natural gas turbines, and hydroelectric dams. They are involved in every aspect of machine operation from determining its optimal positioning in a facility to ensuring it is properly maintained. Their responsibilities include unloading and inspecting new machines using rigging and hoisting devices, assembling machines according to blueprints, and repairing and maintaining equipment. To do their jobs, millwrights use calipers, micrometers, cutting torches, torque wrenches, soldering guns, lathes, and grinding machines. Protective equipment, including safety glasses and hardhats, is required to safeguard against injuries.

Millwrights often work in excess of 40 hours per week, and shift work is common. The job can also require extensive travel—especially for millwrights who specialize in turbine installation, which entails traveling to wind farms and power plants.

Approximately 55,000 millwrights are working in the United States. The majority work for construction firms, although some are employed in the manufacturing, mining, and utilities industries.

Opportunities for millwrights are expected to increase 6 percent by 2016, creating 3,200 new jobs. The BLS predicts that the best opportunities will be in the field of power generation, including wind power and turbines for natural gas plants.

Millwrights need a high school diploma or GED and must complete an apprenticeship program. Apprenticeships last between four and five years and combine classroom instruction with paid on-the-job training.

The Union Millwrights and Machine Erectors (www.unionmillwright.com) and the Millwrights Employers Association (www.machineryinstallers.com) provide information on apprenticeships and union issues.

Millwrights earn a median wage of $21.94 per hour.

Waterpower

Research into the possibilities for harnessing the power of water and transforming it into energy is making waves. Waterpower—which is also referred to as hydropower or hydraulic power—has numerous advantages, including its availability as a nonpolluting renewable power source. Even though hydropower supplies almost 20 percent of the world's electricity, challenges to the installation and maintenance of effective systems, along with the high cost (compared to more traditional sources of electricity), are barriers to waterpower becoming a widely used source of renewable energy. Despite the hurdles, green careers are available in the field and opportunities for growth are expected to soar.

Hydraulic Engineer

Hydraulic engineers research the flow of water and apply their knowledge to the design of bridges, dams, canals, levees, and *hydroelectric power*. To design the components used to create hydroelectric power, hydraulic engineers compute rates of water flow; determine the types of conduits, pumps, and turbines required to transport water and convert it into electricity; devise plans for canals, conduits, and mains necessary to transport and distribute water; and plan reservoirs and booster stations to ensure proper water pressure exists at all levels. Hydraulic engineers also build models to study construction and flow issues, identify issues with hydraulic and pneumatic control devices, and research and test new component functionalities. They might be required to manage workers who are dredging, placing jetties, and constructing levees.

def•i•ni•tion

Hydroelectric power is the electrical energy produced by flowing water. It produces no waste or carbon dioxide—a common greenhouse gas—and is the most widely used source of renewable energy. Currently, hydroelectricity accounts for 19 percent of worldwide electricity production. Canada is the largest producer of hydroelectric power, followed by the United States and Brazil, according to the U.S. Geological Survey (www.usgs.gov).

Hydraulic engineers need a master's degree in hydraulics, hydrology, engineering, or a related field. A Ph.D. might be required for some positions.

The International Association of Hydraulic Engineering and Research (www.iahr.net) is based in Spain but offers conferences around the globe. The association is also a good source of information on issues in hydraulic engineering, including hydroelectric power. The National Hydropower Association (www.hydro.org) and the International Hydropower Association (www.hydropower.org) are good sources of news, job listings, and legislative issues relating to hydropower.

The Hydrologic Engineering Center (www.hec.usace.army.mil) is an organization within the Institute for Water Resources (www.iwr.usace.army.mil) that assists the U.S. Army Corps of Engineers (www.usace.army.mil) in all technical issues related to hydrology. The center offers a number of continuing education classes, including hydraulic engineer role in planning, hydraulic analysis for ecosystem restoration, and statistical methods in hydrology.

Hydraulic engineers earn a median annual salary of $66,260.

Dam Safety Engineer

Dam safety engineers are responsible for the planning, design, construction, operation, and regulation of dams. Their services include performing visual inspections of dams, investigating safety issues, evaluating design and construction procedures, reviewing maintenance records, and making recommendations for remedial measures including the construction of new facilities and the rehabilitation of existing structures. Dam safety engineers are also responsible for preparing and updating emergency action plans and coordinating actions related to dam safety with state and federal agencies.

Inside Scoop

Research shows that dams along the coasts have reduced salmon populations by restricting access to spawning grounds upstream. Salmon are often harmed if they have to pass through turbines during their migration. Dam safety engineers can help mitigate these issues by requiring fish ladders on new projects or as a conditioning of relicensing existing projects. Research is ongoing to design turbines that have less of an impact on aquatic life.

Dam safety engineers also oversee the removal of dams that are no longer in service and develop strategies for addressing any sediment issues. They also make recommendations for the issuance or denial of certificates and permits relating to dam construction and operation.

Dam safety engineers spend a lot of time in the field, traveling to different dams to perform inspections and make recommendations. Overnight travel is often required.

Dam safety engineers need a bachelor's degree in civil engineering, hydrology, or a related field; a master's degree is often the minimum requirement for many positions. Employers also look for candidates with a professional engineering (PE) license.

The Association of State Dam Safety Officials (www.damsafety.org) hosts continuing education classes on a range of dam safety issues, including slope stability for embankment dams and conduits, valves, and gates.

The Hydrologic Engineering Center (www.hec.usace.army.mil) offers continuing education classes in reservoir system analysis and dam safety studies.

Dam safety engineers earn a median salary of $114,210 per year.

Bioenergy

As gas prices continue to soar and concern for the environment intensifies, ethanol and biodiesel have become household words. Currently, corn-based ethanol is the largest source of biofuel in the United States, and recent legislation mandates additional growth of both corn-based biofuels and biofuels from other sources.

Biofuel accounts for just over 1 percent of power and 2 percent of liquid fuel in the United States, but the U.S. Department of Energy (DOE; www.doe.gov) estimates that usage of biofuel could double by 2010 and could grow to as much as 20 percent by 2030, resulting in thousands of new jobs.

Bioenergy Development Manager

Bioenergy development managers identify business and investment opportunities to promote the growth of the *bioenergy* industry. The job entails formulating research plans, establishing relationships with prospective clients and investors, exploring opportunities for product licensing and intellectual property development, and preparing and executing contracts. Bioenergy development managers also oversee project teams that design, model, and optimize process technologies for biofuel development.

def•i•ni•tion

Bioenergy is a form of renewable energy made from biological materials that can be used as fuel. The organic matter can be used as fuel or processed into liquids or gases.

Bioenergy development managers also research legislative requirements for sustainable energy facilities, conduct feasibility studies, and prepare and evaluate applications to finance bioenergy projects.

Travel is an essential part of most positions in this field, especially to Latin America, the Pacific Rim, and Europe.

A minimum of a bachelor's degree in chemical engineering, mechanical engineering, or a related field is necessary to become a bioenergy development manager; most positions require a master's degree.

The median salary for a bioenergy development manager is $140,005 per year.

Biofuel Research Scientist

Biofuel research scientists are responsible for the research and development of *biofuels*. Their responsibilities include researching biochemistry and molecular biology techniques to create enzymes that can be converted to biofuels, investigating the optimization of biofuel production, and improving the stability and product inhibition of engineered enzymes. The job often includes working in protein engineering, cloning and expression of proteins, assay development, and kinetic characterization of proteins.

def•i•ni•tion

Biofuel is derived from agricultural crops. Crops that can be converted into fuel are either high in sugar (sugarcane) or starch (corn) and undergo a fermentation process to produce ethanol. Biofuel can also be made from plants such as soybean and algae that have high amounts of vegetable oil. The oils are heated, reducing their viscosity, and they can be burned directly in a diesel engine. The oils can also be chemically processed to produce biodiesel.

Biofuel research scientists work in labs, conducting experiments, recording the findings of their work, and publishing studies with their results. They might also attend conferences, give presentations, and apply for patents on their work. Jobs are available in laboratories, universities, government agencies, and engineering firms.

There are 87,000 biological scientists in the United States, which includes scientists working in alternative energy research such as biofuels. Although opportunities for biological scientists are expected to increase just 9 percent by 2016, the BLS predicts that growth will remain strong in the area of biofuel research, leading to new job opportunities for scientists in this field.

Biofuel research scientists need a Ph.D. in chemical engineering, biochemistry, or a related field. Some jobs might be available to candidates with a master's degree and significant experience in the biofuel industry.

The National Renewable Energy Laboratory (www.nrel.gov) runs the National Bioenergy Center that offers resources to professionals engaged in biofuel development.

There are also regional biofuels associations, such as the Northwest Biofuels Association (www.nwbiofuels.org); the Southwestern Biofuels Association (www.swbiofuels.org); and the Florida BioFuels Association, Inc. (www.flbiofuel.org), that offer resources, networking opportunities, and events to members.

The median annual salary for a biofuel research scientist is $79,270.

Bioenergy Process Engineer

Bioenergy process engineers oversee the research and development of biofuels. Their role includes identifying technologies for converting biomass to biofuels through fermentation, gasification, and thermochemical routes; exploring new biomass conversion options; and evaluating emerging technologies.

Bioenergy process engineers might also perform calculations such as mass and energy balances and conversion calculations; gather and interpret data; and prepare process flow diagrams, heat and material balances, and piping and instrumentation specifications. They may also be asked to make recommendations for improving unit yields and develop safety, environmental, and strategic refinery projects.

Bioenergy process engineers are expected to experience job growth of 9 percent by 2016. According to the BLS, the best opportunities will be in the area of energy research—particularly the emerging areas of biotechnology and nanotechnology.

A master's degree or Ph.D. in chemical, biological, or biochemical engineering is required to become a bioenergy process engineer.

The Society for the Advancement of Material and Process Engineering (www.sampe.org), the Association of Consulting Chemists and Chemical Engineers (www.chemconsult.org), and the American Institute of Chemical Engineers (www.aiche.org) provide events, continuing education classes, and networking opportunities to members.

The median salary for an energy process engineer is $78,860 per year.

Chemist

Chemists research matter on the atomic and molecular levels to understand how elements join together. Their responsibilities include measuring properties, composition, structure, and reaction rates to understand chemical substances.

In biofuel development, chemists are responsible for pioneering the advancement of biofuel technologies. Their jobs can include performing analyses of *biomass* and its constituents, initiating development activities related to the deconstruction and conversion of *lignocellulosic biomass*, evaluating its chemical and compositional changes, and researching cost-effective options for enzymatic catalysis of lignocellulosic biomass, and its derivatives.

Chemists might also work with other scientists to pioneer research, provide scientific support for patent filings, and prepare research reports based on their findings.

def•i•ni•tion

Biomass is a biological material, such as corn, switchgrass, or oilseed, that can be converted into fuel.

Lignocellulosic biomass is plant biomass composed of cellulose or lignin, such as sawmill discards, municipal paper waste, agricultural residues like sugarcane, and tall grasses, that is converted to ethanol through fermentation.

There are 84,000 chemists in the United States. Almost half of all chemists work in the chemical manufacturing industry; others work for research and development companies or architecture and engineering firms.

The BLS estimates job growth of 9 percent for chemists through 2016, with the bulk of opportunities available to chemists who work in the fields of alternative energy and environmental preservation.

Green Guidance

The newest specialization for chemists is called *green chemistry*. The goal of green chemistry, also called *sustainable chemistry*, is to design chemicals and chemical processes that reduce or eliminate negative environmental impact. The American Chemical Society (www.acs.org) has a Green Chemistry Institute that hosts conferences and networking events and offers awards in the field of green chemistry.

Chemists need a minimum of a bachelor's degree in chemistry or a related field, although most jobs require a master's degree or a Ph.D.

The American Chemical Society (www.acs.org) has events, research, job listings, and other resources for chemists.

The median salary for a chemist is $68,520 per year.

Industrial Truck Driver

Industrial truck drivers transport materials such as biofuel long distances. To do their jobs, industrial truck drivers must check fuel and oil levels in their rigs. They must also inspect trucks to ensure that the brakes, windshield wipers, and lights are in working order and that all required safety equipment, including a fire extinguisher and flares, is on board. They also report when equipment is inoperable, missing, or improperly loaded.

Industrial truck drivers must also follow laws and regulations for delivering biofuel, including unloading into an approved motor fuel dispenser that has been calibrated with the blend of biodiesel being dispensed and providing a bill of lading or other shipment documentation that specifies the amount of biodiesel in the fuel prior to blending.

According to the BLS, 258,000 new jobs for truck drivers are expected to be available over the next decade. As demand for biofuel grows, careers for industrial truck drivers to transport the fuel will grow, too.

Industrial truck drivers often work nights, weekends, and holidays, and most work at least 50 hours per week.

The U.S. Department of Transportation (www.dot.gov) regulates the working conditions of industrial truck drivers who drive interstate routes. The regulations limit the number of hours a driver can be on the road and require drivers to keep logbooks documenting their time. Federal regulations also require industrial truck drivers to be tested for drug and alcohol use, and conduct periodic random tests during their period of employment. To qualify for a job, industrial truck drivers must not have been convicted of a felony involving the use of a motor vehicle or a crime involving drugs, driving under the influence, refusing to submit to an alcohol test, leaving the scene of a crime, or causing a fatality through negligent operation of a motor vehicle. Industrial truck drivers who drive interstate routes must be at least 21 years old and pass a physical exam every two years.

Industrial truck drivers must obtain a commercial driver's license (CDL), which is offered through vocational-technical schools. To qualify for a CDL, applicants must have a clean driving record and pass a written test as well as a road test.

The median wage for an industrial truck driver is $17.41 per hour.

Solar Energy

Solar energy has a bright future. It's a green source of power that has the potential to create more energy in one year than the lifetime energy output of coal, oil, natural gas, and mined uranium combined. The use of solar energy grew 45 percent per year between 2000 and 2007, in part due to the availability of federal tax credits. A growing number of states also require solar energy use as part of their renewable energy standards, leading to even greater demand for the renewable energy source.

Solar energy has the potential to provide two million jobs worldwide by 2020, according to a joint report issued by Greenpeace (www.greenpeace.org) and the European Photovoltaic Industries Association (www.epia.org). Right now, solar companies often find it difficult to hire enough qualified workers to meet consumer demand. Translation: jobs in the field are plentiful.

Solar Engineer

Solar engineers design and develop *solar power* systems. The responsibilities of a solar engineer include conducting site surveys to recommend optimal solar system designs, preparing detailed electrical designs, developing and maintaining solar system documentation, submitting permit applications, providing detailed labor and materials specifications, and conducting site inspections to ensure proper installation on both commercial and residential projects.

def•i•ni•tion

Solar power converts the radiant energy of the sun into electricity. In the United States, 314 megawatts of new solar systems were installed last year, creating more than 6,000 new jobs and adding over $2 billion to the economy, according to the American Solar Energy Industries Association (www.seia.org).

Solar engineers, also called *photovoltaic engineers*, are often called upon by marketing departments to prepare proposals, draft estimates, and execute contracts. They also help resolve technical issues, research new solar technologies, and explore options for designing solar systems that are more efficient.

The position is too new to be tracked by the BLS, but the American Solar Energy Society (www.ases.org) predicts job growth of up to 12 percent over the next decade.

A bachelor's degree in electrical, chemical, or mechanical engineering or in computer science is essential to become a solar engineer; a master's degree improves employment options.

The Solar Energy Industries Association (www.seia.org) and Solar Energy International (www.solarenergy.org) offer workshops, job listings, and resources for solar energy professionals.

The median annual salary for a solar engineer is $73,990.

Market Analyst

Market analysts research the *photovoltaic* market to assess opportunities for growth and investment. The essential job functions of a market analyst include analyzing competing technologies; compiling sales histories, market trends, and market shares to assist solar sales teams in generating sales projections; and creating reports on industry programs.

Some of the main responsibilities of a market analyst include writing briefs, reports, fact sheets, and web postings on solar energy topics; researching and developing positions on legislative and policy issues; and compiling briefs on pertinent news and events. They might also attend trade shows, conferences, and energy commission and trade association meetings, and serve as corporate regulatory representatives.

def•i•ni•tion

Photovoltaic, or PV, is a solar power technology that converts light into energy.

Market analysts need a bachelor's degree in business, policy, environmental studies, or a related discipline. Some companies give preference to candidates with master's degrees.

Professional associations such as the Solar Electric Power Association (www.solarelectricpower.org), the National Renewable Energy Laboratory (www.nrel.gov), and the Solar Energy Industries Association (www.seia.org) provide resources and up-to-date research in the field of solar power.

The median salary for a market analyst is $62,040 per year.

Inside Scoop

Solar Energy International (www.solarenergy.org) reports that on a monthly basis, a one-kilowatt photovoltaic system prevents 150 pounds of coal from being mined, 300 pounds of carbon dioxide from entering the atmosphere, and 105 gallons of water from being consumed.

Solar Installer

Solar installers install solar panels on residential and commercial projects. The job involves traveling from site to site, performing rooftop mounting of racking and solar collectors, installing tanks and other interior equipment, plumbing and wiring all solar equipment, completing system commissioning and operation verification, and finalizing project documentation. As part of their jobs, solar installers handle the preassembly of parts, the unloading of equipment deliveries, and cleanup after installation.

Solar installers work outdoors, often in extreme temperatures. The job requires climbing ladders, working on rooftops, and lifting heavy equipment. Most solar installers work 40 hours per week, although overtime might be expected to finish an installation.

There are no formal educational requirements to become a solar installer, although candidates with electrical, plumbing, and construction experience have an advantage over the competition.

The North American Board of Certified Energy Practitioners (www.nabcep.org) offers several certifications that give solar installers an advantage in the job market, including PV installer certification and solar thermal installer certification, which are geared toward solar installers with some experience in the field. The association also offers an Entry Level Certificate Program for those who want to start their careers as solar installers.

The median wage for a solar installer is $15 per hour.

Solar Sales Associate

Solar sales associates market and sell solar systems to residential and commercial clients. Their responsibilities include prospecting for leads; giving sales presentations on the benefits of solar power; preparing sales quotes; following up with prospective clients; and working with engineering, project management, and operations teams to ensure customer satisfaction.

Inside Scoop
According to the New Jersey Public Interest Research Group (www.njpirg.org), if just 10 percent of homes in the Mid-Atlantic States used some form of solar power, it would create 25,400 jobs by 2014—60 percent of which would be in manufacturing and installation.

The job can involve a great deal of travel. Solar sales associates might travel to prospective client sites and participate in tradeshows to generate sales leads. To meet sales goals, solar sales associates often work in excess of 40 hours per week, including evenings and weekends.

No formal education is required to work as a solar sales associate. Most companies want candidates with proven track records in sales, and experience in the solar industry is a plus.

Solar sales associates often work on commission, so their salaries are linked to their sales numbers.

Geothermal Energy

Geothermal energy is most abundant in areas with volcanoes, geysers, and hot springs. Research into new methods for harnessing this underground energy is making it a viable energy source outside these areas. According to the DOE Energy Efficiency and Renewable Energy Department, geothermal energy could produce 10 percent of U.S. energy needs by 2050, creating 1.7 jobs per megawatt of capacity involved. Geothermal energy plants burn no fuel and generate no emissions, but they do produce an important commodity: careers.

Geothermal Reservoir Engineer

Geothermal reservoir engineers optimize energy extraction from geothermal fields. The job entails monitoring geothermal fields to determine optimal drilling schedules, designing new wells, developing technical solutions to resource and drilling issues, predicting the long-term performance of reservoirs, and evaluating new prospects to develop *geothermal energy*.

def•i•ni•tion

Geothermal energy is generated by heat stored beneath the surface of the earth. It can also find its way to the surface through volcanoes, hot springs, and geysers. The United States produces more thermal energy than any other country in the world. California gets 5 percent of its electricity from geothermal energy.

To do their jobs, geothermal reservoir engineers study field and operational measurement data and use computer models to project the field operations. They spend a lot of time in the field, conducting research and evaluating operations, with the goal of predicting performance and modifying reservoir management for more efficient operation. Geothermal reservoir engineers must also comply with governmental reporting procedures, including environmental rules and policies.

Geothermal reservoir engineers need a minimum of a bachelor's degree in engineering or a related discipline, as well as registration as a licensed PE. However, a graduate degree and a PE license are preferred.

The U.S. DOE has a Geothermal Technologies Program (www.eere.energy.gov/geothermal) that aims to establish geothermal energy as a cost-effective option for U.S. energy supply. The program provides resources to professionals working in the field.

The Geothermal Energy Association (www.geo-energy.org) hosts trade shows and conferences related to geothermal energy. The Association for Women Geoscientists (www.awg.org) is working to increase the participation of women in the geosciences, including geothermal energy.

Geothermal reservoir engineers earn a median annual salary of $84,060.

Geothermal Heat Pump Engineer

A geothermal heat pump engineer installs, maintains, and repairs all the equipment, motors, and electrical components on *geothermal heat pumps*.

def•i•ni•tion

Geothermal heat pumps use a network of buried pipes that are linked to a heat exchanger and ductwork to transfer heat in and out of buildings. Currently, more than 1 million geothermal heat pumps are installed in the United States. According to some estimates, an additional 60,000 heat pumps could be installed every year.

Also called geothermal HVAC engineers, they install, maintain, and repair low- and high-voltage controls, generators, and power transfer switches. Their jobs involve evaluating heat pump operation and performance, identifying equipment needs, and recommending system upgrades. They might also be asked to read electrical schematics and perform minor repairs to the electrical systems on heat pumps.

Geothermal heat pump engineers work with hand tools, measuring devices, milling machines, lathes, welding equipment, and band saws and are responsible for maintaining accurate service logs on all of the work that is performed.

A high school diploma or GED as well as HVAC certification are required for geothermal heat pump engineers. To advance to a management position, a bachelor's degree is required.

The American Society of Heating, Refrigerating and Air-Conditioning Engineers, Inc. (www.ashrae.org) offers several certifications, continuing education classes, and resources for HVAC professionals. The Geothermal Heat Pump Consortium (www.geoexchange.org) also provides industry information to its members.

Geothermal heat pump engineers earn a median salary of $49,860 per year.

Chapter 5

Natural Resources

In This Chapter

- ◆ Careers on the front lines of natural resource conservation

- ◆ Areas of specialization in the field

- ◆ Professional associations that provide networking opportunities, conferences, and job postings

- ◆ Fields in which job opportunities are expected to increase up to 25 percent in the next decade

- ◆ The government agencies that are hiring

Protecting endangered species, conserving forestland, guiding nature hikes, and managing water supplies are all part of working in natural resources management. In this field, workers are directly responsible for protecting and enhancing the environment, working in jobs that have positive impacts on the natural world.

The growing focus on the importance of environmental protection has put a spotlight on protecting natural resources. The 2009 federal budget has allocated more than $9 billion to environmental protection. In addition, the Bureau of Labor Statistics (BLS) predicts strong job growth in most sectors of the industry through 2016, making now a good time to pursue a career in natural resources.

Parks and Recreation

It takes a lot of work to plan, manage, and maintain the parks, recreation areas, playgrounds, and picnic shelters scattered across the United States.

Careers in parks and recreation are as varied as the parks themselves. Jobs are available in rural areas and in big cities; for private corporations or government agencies; working alone in the field or engaged with the public; analyzing technical data or giving educational workshops. Requirements to enter these careers are varied, too. The jobs do have one thing in common, though—they enable workers to combine their careers with their passions for the natural world.

Park Planner

Park planners are responsible for the planning, design, development, and maintenance of parks, trails, and recreational facilities for both new and existing parks. The specific job duties for a park planner can include conducting site analyses, reviewing field survey notes, approving landscape designs, evaluating pricing estimates, coordinating maintenance work, and inspecting completed construction projects. Park planners also ensure that work is performed in accordance with plans, contracts (including bonds and insurance regulations), and city standards.

One of the major responsibilities of a park planner is conducting research on the current and future parks and recreation needs within his jurisdiction. To this end, park planners often facilitate public planning meetings; prepare technical reports; and assess the availability of funding, including the coordination and administration of grants from state and federal agencies.

In the process of planning the development of new parks and the rehabilitation of existing parks, park managers work to protect wetlands, create wildlife habitats in urban areas, and minimize the *heat island effect*. Park managers can also request that picnic shelters, playgrounds, and other park structures be built using eco-friendly and recycled materials.

The majority of park planners work for government agencies, including parks and recreation departments. Securing a job in this field requires a minimum of a bachelor's degree in landscape architecture, park administration, environmental studies, urban planning, or a related field. Most employers also look for candidates who are licensed landscape architects or who are willing to obtain a license within the first year of employment.

The median annual salary for a park planner is $59,560.

def•i•ni•tion

Heat island effect refers to the increase in temperature that occurs over large paved areas, especially in big cities. Natural areas such as forests, parks, and wetlands help to minimize the heat island effect.

One of the biggest environmental consequences of the heat island effect is skyrocketing energy consumption. One report found that the heat island effect costs the city of Los Angeles about $100 million per year in energy use.

Park Manager

Park managers oversee the operations of parks and recreation areas. Their role is to ensure the protection of natural, cultural, and historic resources located within state and national parks. Also called *park directors* or *park superintendents*, park managers inspect facilities like campgrounds, picnic areas, boat ramps, and playgrounds to ensure they are safe and well-maintained. They also identify construction and equipment needs and coordinate volunteer projects throughout the parks. Park managers also act as educators, offering interpretive programs to schools, civic organizations, and community groups.

In the course of managing the day-to-day operations of parks and recreation areas, park managers might take inventory and order equipment, perform routine maintenance projects, coordinate staff schedules (including park patrols), and ensure that all city codes and ordinances are being followed.

Park managers take a lead role in managing the natural resources in parks and recreation areas. Their job is to ensure that visitors have a minimal impact on the ecosystem. To this end, park managers might encourage hikers to follow *Leave No Trace* guidelines, enforce campfire bans, prohibit the use of motorized vehicles on land and water, and close sections of beaches and trails during nesting season.

def•i•ni•tion

Leave No Trace encourages the responsible enjoyment of outdoor recreation areas with minimal impact on the environment. Some of the Leave No Trace (www.lnt.org) principles include visiting in small groups, staying on existing trails, holding on to waste until it can be disposed of properly, and not feeding wildlife.

A bachelor's degree in parks administration or recreation and several years of experience in the field are essential to secure a job as a park manager. Obtaining the Certified Park and Recreation Professional designation through the National Recreation and Parks Association (www.nrpa.org) can boost job options. Candidates for certification require a combination of education and experience.

The median salary for a park manager is $65,111 per year.

Naturalist

Naturalists develop and conduct programming to teach visitors about the natural, historical, and scientific features of parks and recreation districts. They might lead nature walks, offer tours of interpretive centers, teach outdoor education classes, and lead wilderness survival schools. Often, naturalists travel to classrooms and libraries to teach students about the natural areas in the communities.

Developing educational programming is the most important part of the job. To create lessons that are informative and engaging, naturalists tailor programs to various audiences. A program for children can include nature-based crafts, sing-a-longs, and live animals. Adult programming can include audio-visual displays featuring scientific data, interpretive tours, and guest lectures.

Other job duties can include working in visitor centers, coordinating volunteer activities, and assisting with grant writing.

Naturalists are also involved in conservation projects. Their jobs sometimes entail conducting research on animal species in parks; preserving wetlands and wildlife habitats; and working along with other naturalists, park staff, and nonprofit organizations to protect endangered species.

Most naturalists work for regional parks and recreation districts or state parks. Some work for outdoor schools, nature centers, or other nonprofit organizations.

It takes a bachelor's degree in forestry, environmental science, wildlife management, or a related field to become a naturalist. Due to the emphasis on teaching, it's also helpful to complete classes in education.

The Association of Nature Resource Extension Professionals (www.anrep.org) provides networking opportunities, job postings, and annual conferences to its members. Most states also have naturalist associations that offer professional development opportunities and access to local resources.

The median annual salary for a naturalist is $43,118.

Ranger

Rangers are responsible for the care and conservation of parks, forests, and other wild areas. Their goal is to promote recreation, conservation, and environmental stewardship.

Rangers establish and maintain fire controls. To this end, rangers might offer educational programming about fire prevention, post fire warnings, restrict access to high-risk areas, and in case of fire act as first responders.

Providing educational programming is another major component of the job. Rangers might lead hikes, give tours of historic sites, work in visitor centers, and make classroom visits.

Rangers are also responsible for enforcing local, state, and national laws pertaining to wildlife and wildlife conservation. To do this, rangers inspect campsites, investigate complaints, check fishing and hunting licenses, enforce fish and game limits, and assist in search and rescue operations. Their goal is to ensure the protection of wild areas and wildlife.

Inside Scoop

Per year, an estimated 900 million people visit federal lands in the United States alone, according to the U.S. Department of State (www.state.gov). Rangers are needed to protect the natural resources so visitors can continue to enjoy the national forests, parks, recreation sites, wildlife refuges, and nature reserves across the country.

A growing number of rangers are specializing in law enforcement. Called *law enforcement rangers* or *protection rangers*, these rangers are federally commissioned law enforcement officers with the authority to carry weapons, make arrests, and conduct investigations for crimes such as unlawful removal of native plant species and hunting in restricted areas.

Rangers often work for parks, forests, and nature preserves, but the National Park Service (www.nps.gov) also employs rangers to work at national memorials such as the Statue of Liberty. Rangers can also find work in urban parks like Central Park in New York City.

For most positions, a ranger needs a bachelor's degree in forestry, environmental science, or a related field. Law enforcement rangers also need to complete the Seasonal Law Enforcement Training Program (www.anpr.org/academies.htm), which is offered at nine training sites across the United States. Some states require licenses for rangers.

The Association of National Park Rangers (www.anpr.org), the National Parks Conservation Association (www.npca.org), and the Park Law Enforcement Association (www.parkranger.com) offer job boards and networking opportunities.

The median annual salary for a ranger is $40,834.

Fish and Game Warden

Fish and game wardens are responsible for monitoring, preventing, and reporting fish and game law violations. Their job is to patrol hunting and fishing areas, check licenses, enforce catch and game limits, investigate reports of damage to crops by wildlife, aid in prosecuting court cases, and investigate complaints and accidents. Their territories can include lakes, rivers, beaches, wetlands, coastlines, forests, and deserts.

> **Inside Scoop**
>
> Over 25 percent of the world's fish stocks are either overexploited or depleted, according to the UN Food and Agriculture Organization (www.fao.org). Overfishing has caused a 90 percent decline in shark populations; the decline of predators like sharks can have devastating consequences for marine ecology.

In the course of doing their jobs, fish and game wardens might be responsible for seizing fish, game, and related equipment that is in violation of state and federal laws. Enforcing these laws prevents overfishing, which can threaten marine biodiversity, and overhunting, which can lead to species becoming extinct.

Fish and game wardens perform other duties to protect wildlife, including monitoring habitats, protecting nesting sites, and in some cases making recommendations for decreasing the number of animals if overpopulation is a problem.

Fish and game wardens might also conduct educational programs, liaise with other law enforcement agencies, and address public safety concerns related to wildlife.

Some fish and game wardens become wildlife inspectors, working at major ports of entry into the United States to ensure that no fish and wildlife are illegally imported or exported. Others become special agents, or trained criminal investigators, who work undercover to expose illegal practices such as selling the skins of extinct animals.

There are 8,000 fish and game wardens in the United States—a number that is expected to remain flat during the next decade, according to the BLS, due to stagnant federal funding levels.

A bachelor's degree in environmental science, biology, criminal justice, or a related field is essential. Fish and game wardens are also required to attend a training academy that can last from 3 to 12 months, depending on the state.

The U.S. Fish and Wildlife Service (www.fws.gov) maintains a comprehensive list of job openings for fish and game wardens.

The median annual salary for a fish and game warden is $47,830.

> ### Inside Scoop
>
> The states with the highest concentration of fish and game wardens are South Dakota, Montana, Maine, and Idaho. The states that pay the highest wages in the field are Maryland, Washington, South Carolina, and Nevada.

Conservation

Conserving the natural environment ensures that mountains, lakes, forests, and wildlife will be safeguarded for future generations. Concerns over air and water pollution, habitat destruction, climate change, wetlands eradication, and species extinction have boosted funding—and jobs—in the field of conservation.

Careers in this field are about more than just encouraging recycling, resource conservation, and pollution reduction. People employed in conservation are working to reverse the damage and prevent more from happening. In some fields, opportunities are abundant, but in others, it's becoming more difficult to find work.

Ecologist

Ecologists research living things and their relationships to the environment. Ecologists might examine the effects of global warming, rainfall, and pollution on the natural world. Their jobs involve setting up experiments, analyzing data, writing reports, and setting up wildlife management plans.

Ecologists often work with other researchers in the public and private sectors, engineers, urban planners, and government agencies to conduct research and implement positive changes. They implement public outreach activities, such as beach cleanups, and deliver presentations to the scientific community about the findings of their research. On a day-to-day basis, ecologists might locate water and energy resources, assist with remediation at hazardous waste sites, or analyze how forests recover after fire.

Ecologists work for universities, government agencies, and nonprofit organizations. Some are self-employed as consultants who contract their services to help businesses and governments comply with environmental policies on issues such as groundwater decontamination.

Assisting with policy formation is another major focus for ecologists. Their knowledge can help guide laws and regulations that achieve environmental goals, such as minimizing depletion of the ozone layer, preventing the spread of invasive plant species, and protecting fragile wetlands.

The job requires a lot of fieldwork to conduct research and set up experiments. Ecologists sometimes must depend on grant funding for their projects. To this end, the job can require researching and writing grant proposals.

A master's degree in ecology, biology, environmental science, or a related field is essential. The best jobs go to candidates with Ph.D.s.

The median salary for an ecologist is $57,980 per year.

Conservationist

Conservationists manage natural resources to protect them from environmental damage. This job often requires working in isolated areas for long periods of time, performing duties such as planting seedlings, surveying forest areas, and studying erosion. Conservationists partner with government agencies and landowners to develop opportunities to improve land use and protect the environment.

The two main areas of specialization for conservationists are range conservationists and soil and water conservationists.

Range conservationists, also called *range scientists*, manage, improve, and protect rangelands. Their goal is to maximize the use of the land without damaging the environment. To this end, range conservationists might develop resource management plans; restore ecosystems; or study the soil, plants, and animals in the area. Some range conservationists work with ranchers to determine the best animals to graze on the land, the optimum number of animals, and the best seasons for grazing.

Range conservationists play an important role in protecting these areas that contain natural resources such as grasses, wildlife habitats, watersheds, and valuable mineral resources. Due to the landscape, most jobs for range conservationists are in Alaska and in western states such as Montana, Oregon, and Idaho.

Soil and water conservationists, as the title suggests, are concerned with conserving soil, water, and related natural resources. The job can entail providing technical assistance to farmers, forest managers, consulting groups, and government agencies on making productive use of the land while safeguarding the environment. Soil and water conservationists identify erosion problems and work with landowners to develop solutions, research groundwater contamination, or provide suggestions for preserving water supplies.

In all areas of conservation specialization, working conditions are varied. Some conservationists spend most of their time in the field, though others work in offices. Conservationists work for government agencies, consulting companies, universities, and private landowners.

Conservationists need a minimum of a bachelor's degree in ecology, natural resource management, agriculture, environmental science, or a related field. Most jobs require a master's degree or a Ph.D., especially to enter fields such as research and policy development.

The median salary for a conservationist is $57,220 per year.

Green Guidance

The BLS predicts slower-than-average job growth for conservationists due to stagnant funding levels. The best opportunities are expected to be in the fields of soil conservation and erosion.

Restoration Specialist

Restoration specialists support environmental projects such as restoring aquatic habitats, removing invasive plant species, rehabilitating polluted sites, and protecting wildlife areas. They conduct ecological assessments, participate in project planning, and oversee program implementations. They often work in conjunction with nonprofit organizations, developers, and government agencies to develop comprehensive plans for habitat restoration.

Inside Scoop

The National Oceanic and Atmospheric Administration (NOAA) founded the Restoration Center in 1991 (visit their website at www.noaa.gov). It's the only office within NOAA solely devoted to the restoration of coastal, marine, and migratory fish habitats. The Restoration Center employs restoration specialists and other scientists who conduct restoration projects, run a damage assessment and remediation program, raise community awareness about the environmental impacts of marine contamination, and research new technologies to improve restoration efforts.

Restoration specialists divide their time between working in the field conducting research and working in an office designing programs to reverse environmental degradation and destruction. Travel is an expected part of the job.

Increased awareness of the importance of protecting natural areas will benefit restoration specialists. Job opportunities in this field are expected to increase 25 percent by 2016.

To secure a position in this field, a bachelor's degree in biology, microbiology, botany, ecology, or environmental science is required. Many employers look for candidates with a master's degree or a Ph.D.

The Society for Ecological Restoration International (www.ser.org) and the Global Restoration Network (www.globalrestorationnetwork.org) offer continuing education programs, conferences, job listings, and news in the field of environmental restoration.

The median salary for a restoration specialist is $56,100 per year.

Botanist

Botanists research plants and their environments. The job often includes identifying and classifying plants and studying the structure and function of plant parts, the causes and cures of plant diseases, and how plants interact with other organisms and the environment.

Most botanists specialize in a certain group of plants and have titles that reflect their areas of specialization. For example, marine botanists study plants that grow in the ocean, agronomists study agricultural crops and grasses, and taxonomists identify and classify plants.

Inside Scoop

Economic botanists specialize in developing plants into usable products, such as food, drugs, and fibers. Botanists in this area of specialization are partly responsible for the development of clothing made from eco-friendly fibers like soy, hemp, and organic cotton.

According to the Organic Trade Association (OTA), the demand for organic nonfood products such as fiber has grown 26 percent since 2006. Continued demand could boost job opportunities for botanists specializing in this field. Visit the OTA's website at www.ota.com.

Botanists often work for universities; nonprofit organizations; and government agencies such as the U.S. Department of Agriculture, the U.S. Forest Service, and the U.S. Department of the Interior. Some are also employed by museums and botanical gardens.

Job opportunities for botanists are expected to increase as environmental concerns over air, water, and soil pollution continue to mount. A Ph.D. in botany or biology is almost always required to secure a position as a botanist, although it is possible to work as a biological technician with a bachelor's degree.

The Botanical Society of America (www.botany.org) hosts conferences and professional development events and maintains a list of job opportunities for botanists.

The median annual wage for a botanist is $48,000.

Fisheries Manager

Fisheries managers raise fish and shellfish in manufactured environments like ponds, floating net pens, raceways, and recirculating systems. Their job is to stock, feed, and protect marine life. Fisheries managers also oversee the sale of fish and shellfish for consumption and, if applicable, recreational fishing programs offered by fisheries.

def•i•ni•tion

Fisheries often raise specific species of fish and shellfish, such as cod, shrimp, salmon, and catfish. The demand for stocked fish has grown in response to concerns about overfishing and related restrictions on deep-sea fishing, leading to more job opportunities for fisheries managers.

Fisheries, also called aquaculture farms, are established areas where fish species, including shellfish, are raised and caught. The industry employs up to 38 million people worldwide.

Fisheries managers might be responsible for long-term planning of fisheries management programs; directing fisheries investigations on rivers, lakes, tributaries, and reservoirs; reviewing fishing regulations; and making recommendations for changes based on current stock levels.

Inside Scoop

The Marine Stewardship Council (MSC) (www.msc.org) is the world's leading eco-labeling and certification program for seafood raised in sustainable fisheries. The organization aims to reverse the decline of global fish stocks and make improvements in marine conservation.

The MSC's blue label on packaged seafood lets consumers make food choices that support the environment.

Fisheries managers need a bachelor's degree in biology or environmental science with experience in fisheries and aquatic resource management or a master's degree in a related field. Certification as a fisheries scientist by the American Fisheries Society (www.fisheries.org) is desirable.

The median salary for a fisheries manager is $55,651 per year.

Forest Policy Analyst

Forest policy analysts interpret forest-related policies at the regional, national, and international levels and advise on their development and implementation. The job duties include researching the effects of habitat degradation, forest products harvesting, climate change, invasive species, and land use. Forest policy analysts design and complete ecological assessments, review environmental impact statements, develop forest management and conservation plans, and perform field work.

Forest policy analysts might also conduct background research on legal policies involving environmentally harmful forest policies; evaluate the adequacy of local, state, and federal forest regulations; and work with expert witnesses to prepare testimony and technical papers for public meetings and hearings.

Forest policy analysts work for nonprofit organizations, consulting firms, and government agencies.

A master's degree in policy studies, environmental science, forestry, or public administration is necessary to become a forest policy analyst. Certification from the Society of American Foresters (www.safnet.org) can improve job prospects. To qualify, applicants must have a degree coupled with five years of experience and a passing exam grade.

> **Career Crisis**
>
> A lack of federal and state funding means that job growth for forest policy analysts is expected to remain almost flat, increasing only 5 percent by 2016.

The median annual salary for a forest policy analyst is $51,190.

Hydrologist

Hydrologists study water. Their job is to use scientific knowledge and mathematical principles to solve problems with the quantity, quality, and availability of water. Hydrologists might work to control river flooding and erosion, help find water supplies for cities during times of drought, or assist with cleaning up water pollution.

Often, hydrologists specialize in either underground water or surface water. Those who specialize in surface water might test the water quality in estuaries, rivers, and streams to ensure the safety of fish, plants, and wildlife. They might also study the effects of acid rain on wildlife or research how toxic metals in the soil affect aquatic environments.

Hydrologists specializing in underground water, or *groundwater*, might help choose locations for waste disposal sites and monitor the sites to determine whether pollution from the landfill is leaching into the water supplies. They might also measure the volume of water that is stored underground.

The job involves fieldwork to collect data, oversee testing, and conduct experiments, as well as office work to interpret data and perform analyses.

Inside Scoop
The U.S. Geological Survey (www.usgs.gov) estimates that 408 billion gallons of water are used in the United States every year. The two largest uses are power and irrigation. To continue to meet the growing demand for water, hydrologists need to come up with new ways to recycle water and devise manufacturing processes that use less water.

There are approximately 92,000 hydrologists in the Unites States, and the demand is growing rapidly. BLS predicts job growth of 25 percent by 2016 as a result of the increasing demands on water resources. Private consulting firms are expected to be the best places to find jobs.

Currently, most hydrologists work for architectural and engineering firms or consulting services; 28 percent work for the federal government, mostly within the U.S. Department of the Interior and the U.S. Geological Survey; and 21 percent work for state agencies performing geological surveys and working in departments of conservations. A small percentage of hydrologists are self-employed as consultants.

A bachelor's degree in Earth science or environmental science is the minimum requirement to work as a hydrologist. Most employers want candidates with a master's degree in environmental science or hydrology.

The American Institute of Hydrology (www.aihydrology.org) offers additional certification programs in professional hydrology that are beneficial to hydrologists who want to advance in the profession. Median annual earnings of hydrologists are $66,260.

Chapter 6

Sustainable Agriculture

In This Chapter

- ◆ Careers that enable researchers to work hand-in-hand with farmers
- ◆ The field that has more job openings than qualified candidates
- ◆ How to start a career in the fastest-growing field in agriculture
- ◆ Part-time opportunities with huge environmental payoffs
- ◆ Opportunities to bring sustainable agricultural products to consumers

Agriculture has returned to its roots. After a period that emphasized maximizing production through mechanization, chemical use, and specialization, the focus has shifted to meeting national agricultural needs while taking steps to protect the environment. Sustainable agriculture provides innovative and economically viable opportunities for growers, laborers, and consumers. It also addresses the environmental and social costs of traditional farming, such as topsoil depletion, groundwater contamination, and the decline of family farms.

Sustainable agriculture is gaining increasing support, and with its acceptance comes new opportunities for farmers, ranchers, laborers, and researchers that integrate traditional agricultural practices with a modern commitment to the environment.

Research and Development

A lot of behind-the-scenes activities take place to put meat and potatoes on the dinner table. Researchers investigate the best seeds, soil conditions, and pest management techniques; inspectors ensure quality standards are met; and scientists explore the best methods of packaging and shipping every ear of corn and side of beef that ends up on supermarket shelves. The result? Careers that combine science and farming with concern for the environment.

Seed Technologist

Seed technologists research seed varieties and conduct experiments to improve the purity, germination, vigor, and herbicide tolerance. Their goal is to improve the quality of seeds for vegetables, flowers, and grasses. Seed technologists also experiment with new seed hybrids.

Their daily responsibilities include conducting tests to determine the purity and germination levels of various seed types, collecting data, mixing of commercial and experimental seed compounds, implementing field testing, managing seed inventories, and overseeing lab operations.

In an effort to conserve resources and minimize the application of toxic chemicals in the field, some seed technologists are specializing in developing seed hybrids that are drought-tolerant and resistant to pests and diseases.

Seed technologists work in labs, colleges and universities, seed companies, and research firms. The job requires a minimum of a bachelor's degree in seed technology, agronomy, horticulture, or a related field; however, a master's degree is preferred.

The Society of Commercial Seed Technologists (www.seedtechnology.net) and the Association of Official Seed Analysts (www.aosaseed.com) offer continuing education classes to keep seed technologists up-to-date on advancements in the field.

The median annual salary for seed technologists is $62,970.

Crop Scientist

Crop scientists research and advise on all aspects of crop health. Their goal is to provide the most cost-effective and environmentally sound ways to manage all aspects of crop health.

The day-to-day responsibilities of crop scientists include assessing the health and suitability of agricultural land, researching new ways to grow crops, developing new pesticides and herbicides, and conducting studies on environmental conditions. Some crop scientists also teach seminars on effective crop management for farmers.

Crop scientists play an important role in environmental protection. They might educate farmers on the importance of soil conservation and crop rotation; develop nontoxic fertilizers, herbicides, and pesticides; and advocate for efficient irrigation practices. In some cases, crop scientists are called on to provide assessments and information about the health of crops on farms and government testing laboratories.

Crop scientists work for colleges and universities, government agencies, and farming associations; some also work as consultants, advising ranchers and farmers on the best options for their livestock and crops. The job can require long hours and extensive travel, especially for crop scientists who consult with farmers in various parts of the country.

A minimum of a bachelor's degree in agriculture or Earth science is necessary to become a crop scientist. The best opportunities are available to those with a master's degree in crop science, botany, biology, or a related field.

The Crop Science Society of America (www.crops.org) and the American Society of Agronomy (www.agronomy.org) provide job listings, conferences, and continuing education programs in the field of crop science.

The median salary for a crop scientist is $48,670 per year.

Soil Scientist

Soil scientists examine the physical, chemical, and biological properties of soil and use their research to solve environmental problems. Their work can be used to promote crop growth, control erosion, and conserve wetlands. Soil scientists, also called *soil analysts* or *soil conservationists*, are also asked to assist with *bioremediation*, evaluate the environmental impact of landfills, and advise on effective land use.

def•i•ni•tion

Bioremediation is the use of living organisms such as bacteria to clean up oil spills or remove other pollutants from soil, water, and wastewater.

The job duties of a soil scientist can include conducting soil surveys, classifying soil types, interpreting soil test results, analyzing soil requirements, and selecting soil amendments.

Growing concern for the environment has improved career opportunities for soil scientists. They are being called on to help improve agricultural output while preserving soil and water. To achieve this goal, soil scientists are developing plans to manage soil fertility and erosion without using harmful chemicals.

Most soil scientists work for engineering and consulting firms; the federal government, universities, and nonprofit organizations also hire soil scientists.

There are 16,000 soil scientists in the United States. Opportunities are expected to increase 8 percent by 2016. According to the U.S. Bureau of Labor Statistics (BLS), candidates with graduate degrees and experience in environmental preservation have the best opportunities. A master's degree in science, engineering, or a related field is essential to work as a soil scientist, although a Ph.D. is recommended.

The Soil Science Society of America (www.soils.org) offers accreditation as a Certified Professional Soil Scientist/Classifier. Applicants must have a degree in soil science or related field with five years of experience, or a master's degree and three years of experience; they also must pass written exams and agree to a code of ethics. Continuing education classes are required to maintain the certification.

The National Society of Consulting Soil Scientists (www.nscss.org) hosts an annual conference and offers up-to-date research and information in the field of soil science.

The median annual salary for a soil scientist is $56,080.

Integrated Pest Management Specialist

Integrated pest management (IPM) specialists are responsible for managing pests using the least invasive and most economical methods available. IPM specialists advise on methods for preventing infestation such as crop rotation, selecting pest-resistant plant and seed varieties, and planting pest-free rootstock. They also advocate for controlling pests using green pest control techniques like pheromones to disrupt pest mating as well as noninvasive controls, including trapping and weeding. They also participate in raising beneficial insects.

def•i•ni•tion

> **Integrated pest management (IPM)** is an environmentally sensitive approach to pest management that aims to reduce and/or eliminate the use of pesticides.

Some of the main duties of IPM specialists include monitoring pest populations; assessing various options for pest control, including mechanical, biological, and chemical controls; and setting action thresholds to determine the point when pest populations or environmental conditions require intervention.

IPM specialists can work for crop consulting firms, chemical and seed manufacturers, research laboratories, horticultural production companies, and colleges and universities.

The field of integrated pest management is too new for the BLS to collect occupational information. According to the University of Illinois at Urbana-Champaign, there are more job openings than qualified candidates in the field of integrated pest management.

Integrated pest management specialists need a bachelor's degree in crop science, agriculture, plant biology, or a related field. Opportunities are best for candidates with master's degrees.

The IPM Institute of North America (www.ipminstitute.org) offers classes, resources, and job opportunities in the field of integrated pest management.

The median annual salary for an IPM specialist is $56,080.

Agricultural Inspector

Agricultural inspectors are responsible for inspecting agricultural commodities, processing equipment, and facilities like farms and fisheries to ensure compliance with laws and regulations governing health and safety. Their jobs can entail collecting samples of agricultural products and sending them to the lab to test for contamination, weighing and inspecting agricultural shipments that are being imported or exported, and visiting logging sites to ensure that safety regulations are being enforced.

Agricultural inspectors also review the records of producers, processors, and handlers of Certified Organic agricultural products, such as plants, animals, food, and fibers, to ensure they conform with the requirements of the United States Department of Agriculture's National Organic Program.

The largest employers of agricultural inspectors are federal, state, and local governments; management firms; agents and brokers; and universities.

Currently, 16,000 agricultural inspectors are working in the United States. According to BLS, businesses are being required to conduct their own inspections, leading to a decline in the number of new jobs for agricultural inspectors. Opportunities in the field are expected to remain flat for the next decade.

> **Inside Scoop**
>
> The states with the highest concentrations of agricultural inspectors are Arkansas, Nebraska, Iowa, and Delaware. Agricultural inspectors can earn the highest salaries in Connecticut, New York, New Jersey, North Dakota, and Michigan.

Agricultural inspectors need a bachelor's degree in agricultural science or a related field.

The National Association of State Departments of Agriculture (www.nasda.org) offers continuing education courses.

The median salary for an agricultural inspector is $39,830 per year.

Food Scientist

Food scientists research new methods for preserving and processing foods, discovering new food sources, analyzing food content, making decisions about food packaging, and enforcing government regulations. Some food scientists focus on the science behind various food processing, baking, canning, blanching, and pasteurization methods. Food scientists also might lead expert panels or studies that evaluate various food products.

As a result of the increased awareness of the harmful effects of preservatives, a growing number of food scientists are exploring options for removing food additives and researching alternatives for additives such as nitrates.

Food scientists work for colleges, research companies, and food processing plants. Their jobs can require working in test kitchens or laboratories.

There are 12,000 food scientists in the United States, and job opportunities are expected to increase just 9 percent by 2016. BLS attributes the lack of opportunities to decreased federal funding for research positions in food science. In this employment arena, the best opportunities will be available in the private sector, where demand for new food products and enhanced food safety measures will spur job growth.

Food scientists need a bachelor's degree in food science, nutrition, or a related field. Research positions require a master's degree.

The Institute of Food Technologists (www.ift.org) provides resources for food scientists.

Food scientists earn a median annual wage of $53,810.

Organic Farm Certification Specialist

Organic farm certification specialists are responsible for reviewing and processing applications from farmers seeking organic farm certification. They perform onsite inspections, communicate requirements to farmers, examine all aspects of farm operations, take random samples to test for chemicals, and grant certifications to farms that meet the requirements of the United States Department of Agriculture National Organic Standards Program (www.ams.usda.gov). They also perform annual scheduled inspections of organic farms as a requirement for maintaining certification.

Inside Scoop

Organic farming has been one of the fastest-growing segments of U.S. agriculture for more than a decade. In 1990, when Congress first passed the Organic Foods Production Act, one million acres of Certified Organic farmland existed. Today, that number tops four million acres. California, Wisconsin, and Washington have more Certified Organic farms than any other states in the country.

The job requires extensive travel and is often a part-time position. Candidates who speak both English and Spanish are sometimes given preference.

The best opportunities are available to organic farm certification specialists with two-year degrees in agriculture, environmental science, and food science.

The Independent Organic Inspectors Association (www.ioia.net) offers training for certification specialists. California Certified Organic Farmers (www.ccof.org) is an international association that also offers accreditation for certification specialists.

The average wage for an organic farm certification specialist is $12 per hour.

Large-Scale Farming

A mere 10 percent of the farms in the United States are considered large-scale farming operations. Even so, farmers and ranchers who raise wheat, corn, cattle, and livestock on large farms account for 75 percent of the agricultural output in the United States, according to the U.S. Department of Agriculture (www.usda.gov).

Some large farms specialize in a single crop, whereas others produce multiple agricultural products. There is one common practice among large-scale farming operations—a shift toward more sustainable farming practices, leading to a growth in the number of green careers available to farmers and other agricultural workers.

Organic Farmer

Organic farmers are responsible for all aspects of farm operations from planting and harvesting crops to managing pests and selling produce. The goal of organic farming is to have minimal impact on the environment. To do this, organic farmers forgo synthetic fertilizers, livestock feed additives, chemical pesticides, and genetically modified organisms.

Inside Scoop

The market for organic products has grown an average of 25 percent per year since 1990 to become a $33 billion market. Currently, more than 633,000 Certified Organic farms are in operation around the world. The countries with the highest number of Certified Organic farms are Australia, Argentina, China, and the United States, according to "The World of Organic Agriculture," a report by the International Federation of Organic Agriculture Movements (www.ifoam.org).

Organic farmers raise agricultural crops such as wheat, corn, potatoes, soybeans, apples, and other fruits and vegetables. They decide which crops to plant, order seeds and plant starts, prepare the soil, manage pests and weeds, harvest crops, and oversee sales and distribution. Their jobs also involve negotiating with lenders to finance equipment, livestock, and seed; hiring and supervising farmhands; and repairing and maintaining farm machines.

Organic farmers rotate crops, fertilize with compost, use biological pest control, and harvest crops manually.

Organic farmers might opt to have their farms Certified Organic in accordance with United States Department of Agriculture National Organic Standards Program. Their produce is often sold to cooperatives, food processing plants, and grocers. The majority of organic farmers sell their produce directly to the public at farmers' markets, u-pick farms, and farm stands.

There are 1.3 million farmers and ranchers in the United States. Opportunities are expected to decline 8 percent by 2016, due to increased mechanization and increased costs for farmland and equipment. Despite the overall decline in opportunities for farmers, the BLS reports that organic farming is the fastest-growing segment in agriculture.

Green Guidance

Corporations and large farming conglomerates are better able to withstand fluctuations in income and agricultural output. They are also more successful in securing government subsidies that are often based on the number of acres owned and per-unit production. As a result, small family farms are disappearing while large-scale farming operations are hiring more agricultural workers.

Organic farmers are self-employed. They put in long hours, often working from sunrise to sunset. The job entails working evenings and weekends, with limited time off during planting, growing, and harvesting seasons.

Organic farmers might have a bachelor's degree in agriculture or farm management, although on-the-job training is still the most common way to learn the trade.

Several states have organic farming associations that help members stay up-to-date on the latest trends, provide assistance with marketing, and offer networking opportunities.

Salaries for organic farmers depend on a number of factors, including prices of farm products (which rise and fall depending on factors like the weather), farm output, and consumer demand. A farm that shows large profits one year can experience a loss the following year.

On average, organic farmers earn a median annual income of $42,480.

Organic Rancher

Organic ranchers raise cattle using humane practices that have minimal impact on the environment. They allow cattle to roam free (called *free range*), rotate their grazing between fields to prevent soil erosion, and do not inject them with hormones or antibiotics. Ranchers also schedule regular vet appointments and oversee the breeding of their livestock.

> **Inside Scoop**
>
> Confining cattle in small spaces can lead to the spread of diseases such as mad cow disease. Animals that are confined in small spaces also create a lot of waste that can overflow and seep into the soil and water in the surrounding environment.

Organic ranchers select pasture to graze animals; observe animals to detect illness or injury; attend to animals during and after birth; castrate their herds; and oversee animal identification such as branding, tattooing, and tagging. They also clean barns and stalls, repair fences and pens, and maintain farm machinery and equipment.

Organic ranching requires more space, so organic ranchers tend to farm on a smaller scale than conventional ranchers. Like organic farmers, organic ranchers sell meat to food processing plants, cooperatives, and grocers. A growing number of organic ranchers are selling meat at farmers' markets.

Organic ranchers are often self-employed, although some may work as agricultural managers for large ranches. The job requires long hours, including night and weekend work—especially if organic ranchers have to go to the barn in the middle of the night to attend to birthing livestock.

Most organic ranchers learn on the job, although some have bachelor's degrees in agriculture or farm management.

The Society for Range Management (www.rangelands.org) offers accreditation as a Certified Professional in Range Management and Certified Range Management Consultant, as well as continuing education classes in the field of range management.

The median annual salary for an organic rancher is $33,360.

Organic Dairy Manager

Organic dairy farmers raise dairy cows using humane practices that have minimal impact on the environment. In an organic herd, dairy cows are not given hormones or antibiotics and graze on farmland that has not been treated with pesticides.

Organic dairy managers oversee the day-to-day operations of commercial dairies. Their jobs include purchasing feed and supplies, managing herd health and reproduction, and training and supervising farmhands.

One of the main roles of an organic dairy manager is overseeing milking operations. To this end, they ensure cattle are milked on a regular basis, process the raw material, store the finished product, and oversee packaging—all while ensuring that the process is in compliance with regulatory agencies and quality assurance programs. They also maintain milking equipment, plan production schedules to ensure enough milk is produced to fill orders, and implement effective product rotation schedules to provide code dates for sales and distribution.

Dairy managers produce organic milk for food processing plants, co-ops, and supermarkets where it is sold as milk, cheese, yogurt, and other organic dairy products. Increasingly, dairy managers are also selling organic milk directly to the public through farmers' markets.

The U.S. Department of Agriculture does not track the number of organic dairy farms, making it difficult to assess their prevalence in the United States. According to the Organic Trade Association, dairy is one of the fastest-growing segments of the organic foods industry, with sales topping $1.3 billion last year. In fact, demand for organic milk has been growing by more than 20 percent per year, creating frequent shortages in dairy cases across the country—and more opportunities for organic dairy farmers.

Dairy managers are employed by large dairies and often work long hours, including evenings and weekends. To supervise farmhands from diverse backgrounds, it's helpful to speak both English and Spanish.

A bachelor's degree in dairy science or a related field is helpful to secure a position, although some dairy farmers hire dairy managers with a high school diploma and experience working on a dairy farm.

The Northeast Organic Dairy Producers Alliance (www.organicmilk.org) provides resources for dairy farmers in the northeast United States who run organic dairies or want to transition traditional dairies into organic operations.

The median annual wage for a dairy farmer is $42,480.

Organic Livestock Manager

Organic livestock managers oversee all aspects of livestock. Their responsibilities include the feeding and watering, vaccinations, castration, branding, and breeding of livestock such as pigs, sheep, goats, and chickens. Organic livestock managers also sheer sheep; handle barn and pasture maintenance; and maintain records regarding the weights, diets, birth records, and pedigrees of their animals.

Animals are sold for food, hides, and breeding. To ensure the farms have minimal impact on the environment and livestock are treated in a humane manner, organic livestock managers allow animals to graze in open fields, rotate animals between pastures, and avoid the use of antibiotics and hormones. They also follow government-enforced humane laws, such as limited de-beaking on chickens.

Inside Scoop

On conventional livestock farms, almost 24 million pounds of antibiotics—about 70 percent of the antibiotics used in the United States—are added to animal feed every year to speed livestock growth, according to the Natural Resources Defense Council (www. nrdc.org). These antibiotics end up in the animal manure that is used to fertilize crops, contaminating foods with antibiotic residue.

Organic livestock managers, as the title suggests, work for organic livestock farms. Some work at farms with multiple kinds of animals, including chickens, sheep, and goats; others work on livestock-specific farms, like pig farms. Regardless of the type of farm, the hours are long and the job requires evening and weekend work, especially during breeding season.

The BLS predicts that jobs in agricultural management, including livestock management, will increase just 1 percent by 2016, creating approximately 3,000 new jobs nationwide. The increase is due, in part, to a growing number of landowners living offsite and hiring livestock managers to oversee the farms in their absence.

Organic livestock managers learn the trade through on-the-job training, although some have bachelor's degrees in livestock technology, agricultural science, animal husbandry, or a related field.

The American Society of Farm Managers and Rural Appraisers (www.asfmra.org) offers certification as an Accredited Farm Manager that can boost job opportunities.

The National Livestock Producers Association (www.nlpa.org) offers networking opportunities and funding options through the livestock marketing initiatives and credit cooperatives.

Several other livestock associations assist members with marketing efforts, auctions, exporting, and continuing education. A few of the largest associations include Producers Livestock Marketing Association (www.producerslivestock.com), Livestock Exporters Association of USA (www.livestockexporters-usa.com), and Equity Cooperative Livestock Sales Association (www.equitycoop.com).

The median annual salary for an organic livestock manager is $52,052.

Fisheries Scientist

Fisheries scientists manage fish populations in reservoirs, lakes, rivers, and aquaculture facilities. Their duties include conducting research on fish populations and aquatic ecosystems, developing strategies for marine conservation, providing sustainability assessments for seafood, and advising marine programs on aquaculture issues.

On a daily basis, fisheries scientists may analyze data, prepare and deliver technical presentations, and performs field investigations. Their overall goal is to preserve and protect marine ecosystems.

Fisheries scientists work for federal and state agencies, consulting firms, reclamation companies, commercial fisheries and hatcheries, and at aquaculture farms. Some fisheries scientists also hold academic positions or work for nonprofit organizations such as environmental advocacy groups, nature centers, and zoos.

> **Inside Scoop**
>
> Almost one billion people around the world rely on fish as their primary source of protein—and half of that is produced by fish farms, according to the National Oceanic and Atmospheric Administration (www.noaa.gov).

The aquaculture industry has experienced an average annual growth rate of 8.8 percent since 1970, making it the fastest-growing source of food production in the world, according to the U.N. Food and Agriculture Organization. Concerns about overfishing and the depletion of the stock of certain wild fish species, combined with growing awareness of marine pollution, have created opportunities for fisheries scientists.

Fisheries scientists require a minimum of a bachelor's degree in biology, aquaculture, or a related field. Some employers require candidates to have a master's degree or Ph.D.

The American Fisheries Society (www.fisheries.org) offers two certifications—Associate Fisheries Professional and Certified Fisheries Professional—as well as job listings and other industry resources.

The Global Aquaculture Alliance (www.gaalliance.org) oversees the Responsible Aquaculture Program to ensure best practices in the field.

The median salary for a fisheries manager is $62,000 per year.

Small-Scale Farming

Small farms are the backbone of the U.S. farming industry. The U.S. Department of Agriculture (www.usda.gov) reports that small farms (with less than $250,000 per year in sales) account for 90 percent of farms in the country and 61 percent of the total farmland in the United States. The struggle for small farms to survive has led to the advent of several creative marketing strategies, including more direct sales to customers through events like farmers' markets. Consumer demand has also led small-scale agriculturalists to expand their organic offerings to bolster sales. The switch to grassroots efforts to produce, harvest, package, and market agricultural products has created a bounty of green-collar jobs.

Community-Supported Agriculture Coordinator

Community-supported agriculture (CSA) coordinators oversee the production, distribution, and delivery of agricultural crops to shareholders. CSA coordinators assist with the development of CSA programs, market the programs to possible members, sign up shareholders, manage all aspects of weekly produce deliveries, process payments, and answer questions from shareholders. One of the main roles of the CSA coordinator is monitoring share values and adjusting the volume and selection of crops based on the season and number of shareholders. The job can also include guiding farm tours, writing monthly newsletters, coordinating volunteers, and working at special events like farmers' markets.

def•i•ni•tion

> **Community-supported agriculture (CSA),** also called *subscription farming,* allows members to purchase shares in a local farm in exchange for regular, often weekly, deliveries of farm products such as fruits, herbs, flowers, nuts, eggs, milk, and meat during the growing season. The concept was developed in Europe as a means of supporting local farms. It was introduced in the United States in the 1980s and has grown to include more than 2,000 farms across the country.

On small farms, farmers partner with each other to offer shareholders a more diverse selection of produce or year-round delivery. In these cases, CSA coordinators might be asked to develop relationships with nearby farms and work with other CSA coordinators to plan and schedule deliveries.

CSA coordinators work for farmers, often in offices located on farmland. In the United States, the bulk of CSA farms are located near cities in the northeast, the Great Lakes region, and along the West Coast, although opportunities are available throughout the country as well as in Canada, Europe, and Japan.

Most CSA coordinators work fewer than 40 hours per week and, depending on the farm, the job might be seasonal. The hours are often typical business hours, although some positions require evening and weekend work—especially if CSA coordinators are needed to staff a booth at the farmers' market or to lead farm tours.

A high school diploma is the minimum requirement to work as a CSA coordinator. Some positions might require a bachelor's degree in agriculture or a related field.

The median wage for a CSA coordinator is $12 per hour.

Community Garden Coordinator

Community garden coordinators are in charge of the operation of local community gardening programs. Community garden coordinators are responsible for marketing the programs to prospective members; processing applications and payments for the rental of garden plots; coordinating special events, including gardening workshops; recruiting and training volunteers; and securing donations of seeds, soil, and other garden equipment. They also ensure that all areas of the garden are safe and well maintained, respond to gardener questions, and provide information on eco-friendly weed and pest control methods. In some community gardens, members opt to donate excess produce to local food programs or sell their produce at farm stands, in which case community garden coordinators are responsible for managing these efforts.

def•i•ni•tion

Community gardens rent garden shares to members, allowing them to grow fruits, vegetables, and flowers on public land while sharing resources with other members. More than 5,000 community gardens exist in the United States, according to the American Community Gardening Association (www.communitygarden.org). The benefits of community gardening range from fostering community development and encouraging self-reliance to conserving resources and creating opportunities for environmental education.

Community garden coordinators often work for parks and recreation departments and nonprofit organizations that own the land and oversee the programs. The job is often seasonal and requires evening and weekend hours, especially during peak growing season.

Community garden coordinators need a high school diploma; a bachelor's degree in horticulture or a related field might be necessary for some positions.

The median salary for a community garden coordinator is $31,500 per year.

Winemaker

Winemakers are responsible for all aspects of winemaking operations, from managing harvest activities and overseeing fermentation activities to meeting production schedules and coordinating tastings. The daily duties of a winemaker include making decisions about crushing, pressing, and fermentation; sampling blends and making recommendations for juice and wine additions; performing fining and oak trials; creating wine flavor profiles; monitoring cellar operations to ensure production schedules are met; and overseeing record keeping for legal compliance with federal and state regulations. Winemakers also supervise and train support staff, including assistant winemakers, enologists, and seasonal workers.

Inside Scoop

The knowledge that grapes are among the most pesticide-laden produce has led to a thriving market for organic wines. In the United States, sales of Certified Organic wine and wines made from organic grapes hit $80 million last year—a 28 percent increase since 2004, according to the Organic Trade Association (www.ota.com). Demand is expected to continue to grow at a rate of 17 percent per year over the next five years.

On organic vineyards, winemakers follow strict standards, including the use of natural predators instead of pesticides and using compost for fertilizer, to create *organic wines*. Additionally, winemakers assist in choosing crops that are suitable for the local environment.

def•i•ni•tion

> **Organic wines** have the U.S. Department of Agriculture seal to indicate that they are made with ingredients that are 100 percent organic. Organic wines are different from wines labeled, "made with organic grapes," which means the grapes are organic but additives might have been introduced during the winemaking process.

During a typical workday, winemakers divide their time between vineyards, laboratories, and wine cellars. Most winemakers work 40 hours per week, although overtime is common during harvest season and weekend work is common, especially for tastings and other special events.

Vineyards are scattered across the country, although jobs are most plentiful in established wine-growing regions such as California, Oregon, Washington, and Ohio.

Winemakers need a bachelor's degree in fermentation science, enology, viticulture, or a related field.

Several regional associations provide resources, events, and networking opportunities for professional winemakers.

Winemakers earn a median annual salary of $55,932.

Beekeeper

Beekeepers raise bees to collect honey and beeswax, pollinate crops, or produce bees to sell to other beekeepers. Beekeepers, also called *apiarists*, set hives in orchards and near other sources of nectar and pollen to promote pollination. They might also sell queen bees and cultivate bees for colonies. The job involves assembling beehives, inserting honeycombs, scraping out parasites like wax moth larvae, destroying diseased bee colonies, extracting honey from harvested honeycombs, and collecting *royal jelly* from queen bee cells.

def•i•ni•tion

Royal jelly is a glandular secretion produced by young bees that is high in vitamin B, amino acids, unsaturated fats, and minerals. It is a natural ingredient used in dietary supplements and beauty products.

Some beekeepers make their livings providing pollination services to farmers, which requires migrating with the seasons. In the spring, they travel to warmer climates, such as Florida and California, to make early honey and pollinate almond groves, and to northern states in the summer to pollinate tree fruits and berries. Other beekeepers earn income selling hive products such as honey and beeswax.

Most beekeepers are self-employed, although some work for farm bureaus, parks and recreation districts, and agricultural companies. During peak season (from June to October) beekeepers work longer hours, including weekends.

Inside Scoop

The honeybee population is steadily declining, falling nearly 30 percent over the past 25 years due, in part, to an Asian mite that sucks the juices out of the honeybees and cripples entire colonies. According to a report issued by the National Academies (www.nationalacademies.org), the losses could have huge impacts on farmers across the United States, who spend approximately $150 million per year to rent hives to pollinate their crops.

Farmers in the United States pay about $150 million a year to rent hives, and demand is growing.

There are no formal educational requirements to become a beekeeper; most learn through on-the-job training.

The American Beekeeping Federation (www.abfnet.org) offers a wealth of resources to professional beekeepers. Most states also have regional beekeeping associations.

Salaries for beekeepers depend on weather conditions, production costs, and the current market value of honey. Their median annual salary is $28,000.

Retail Sales and Distribution

Careers in retail sales and distribution are essential to the success of sustainable agriculture. After eco-friendly products are produced, they have to find their way to store shelves. As demand for organic, locally produced, and free-range products continues to grow, farmers' market managers, produce managers, and butchers are vital to making them available to consumers. In this field, workers also play a lead role in educating consumers about the difference between traditional farming methods and sustainable agriculture, with the goal of increasing demand for products that minimize environmental impact.

Farmers' Market Manager

Farmers' market managers are responsible for the overall operation of local farmers' markets. Their job duties include recruiting vendors; collecting payments; ensuring efficient market operations; and promoting the seasonal, locally grown products sold at the markets.

Farmers' markets often run on weekends and evenings during the week. During market operations, farmers' market managers need to be onsite to answer vendor questions, uphold market rules and regulations, and assess attendance levels. They also plan and implement special events, such as cooking demonstrations and musical entertainment.

Farmers' markets are often nonprofit organizations that operate markets in local communities. Market managers divide their time between traditional office settings and the actual markets. Some market managers work 40 hours per week, including evenings and weekends during the growing season, while others are employed on a part-time basis.

> ### Inside Scoop
>
> The number of farmers' markets grew from 1,755 in 1994 to more than 4,385 in 2007, according to the U.S. Department of Agriculture (www.usda.gov), creating more job opportunities for market managers.

Farmers' market managers do not need formal education, although a bachelor's degree can be helpful.

The North American Farmers' Market Direct Marketing Association (www.nafdma.com) offers networking opportunities for farmers' market managers. Most states also have regional farmers' market associations that provide resources and events for members.

The median salary for a farmers' market manager is $29,120 per year.

Produce Manager

Produce managers run the produce departments in supermarkets, food co-ops, specialty grocers, and big box stores. Their responsibilities include developing relationships with suppliers, ordering fruits and vegetables, assisting customers with produce selection, and resolving complaints about merchandise quality. Produce managers also manage inventory and pricing to achieve required profit margins and create attractive in-store produce displays. In some cases, produce managers also supervise and train employees who work in the produce department.

Produce managers play a lead role in selecting and stocking organic and locally grown produce. Some produce managers might work for grocers who specialize in selling organic produce.

> **Inside Scoop**
>
> Wal-Mart (www.walmart.com) is the nation's largest buyer of locally grown fruits and vegetables. The retailer began selling organic produce in 2006, with the goal of becoming the largest mass-market provider of organic foods. In 2008, Wal-Mart announced plans to buy and sell $400 million worth of produce grown by local farmers in its state stores.

The job often requires working evenings and weekends, and overtime might be necessary when produce shipments arrive.

There are no formal educational requirements to become a produce manager, although most employers require a state-issued food handler card.

The National Grocers Association (www.nationalgrocers.org) hosts conferences and educational programs and provides information on industry trends to members.

Produce managers earn a median salary of $36,200 per year.

Butcher

Butchers prepare cuts of meat, such as steaks, chops, roasts, and ground meat, for supermarkets, restaurants, and wholesalers. The job involves using tools like knives and cleavers; weighing, wrapping, and labeling cuts of meat; displaying meat in refrigerated cases; and fulfilling customer requests. Butchers can work for specialty stores where the meats are organic, free range, and grass-fed.

Butchers might work in butcher shops, supermarkets, meatpacking plants, hotels, restaurants,
and slaughterhouses. To prevent meat from
spoiling, butchers often work in refrigerated
rooms. Butchers are more susceptible to injury
than workers in other industries, according to
the BLS. Working with knives, cleavers, and
power tools can cause injuries ranging from
minor cuts to amputations. Slicing meat can
also cause repetitive stress injuries such as
carpal tunnel syndrome.

Inside Scoop
Organic meat is the fastest-growing segment of the organic foods business, according to the Agricultural Marketing Resource Center (www.agmrc.org). Sales grew 67.4 percent last year, topping $114 million.

Currently, 131,000 butchers are working in the United States. As a result of increased
automation, opportunities are expected to increase only 2 percent by 2016.

Butchers learn their skills on the job; a high school diploma is the minimum requirement for most positions.

Butchers earn a median annual salary of $28,840.

Chapter 7

Waste Management

In This Chapter

◆ Details on the waste management career that is expected to experience 25 percent job growth by 2016

◆ Government legislation that is impacting jobs in this field

◆ Dangers associated with working in certain waste management careers

◆ Entry-level employment opportunities for job seekers with high school diplomas

"Reduce, reuse, recycle" is the mantra of green living—and careers in waste management revolve around putting it into practice.

Consider this: the average American produces 56 tons of trash per year and only one-tenth of it is recycled. To complicate matters, over the past 16 years, the number of landfills in the United States has dropped 84 percent; during the same time period, an 80 percent increase has occurred in the amount of trash generated.

Careers in waste management extend beyond trash collection. In addition to jobs for landfill planners and recycling center supervisors, opportunities also exist for environmental engineers, soil scientists, and greenhouse gas engineers, making occupations in waste management as varied as the trash that ends up in the landfill.

Keeping It Clean

Dealing with trash is dirty business. It's not just the number of milk cartons and plastic bags in the landfills that requires attention; it takes a team of experts to research, analyze, and monitor landfills and recycling centers before a single candy wrapper or aluminum can is tossed.

There is a science behind selecting a landfill site and assessing its environmental impact, measuring pollution, and studying how trash affects the soil and water. Efforts to keep the environment clean can involve getting dirty, but the payoff is strong job growth, above-average salaries, and the promise of a safer environment.

Environmental Engineer

Environmental engineers develop solutions to environmental issues such as water contamination, air pollution, and waste disposal. Their jobs might include researching the environmental impacts of proposed construction sites, designing wastewater treatment facilities, or advising on the treatment and containment of hazardous waste. Environmental engineers are also involved in *bioremediation*.

def•i•ni•tion

Bioremediation uses living organisms to clean up contaminated soil or water. Using nitrate and/or sulfate fertilizers to clean up oil spills is one example of bioremediation.

On a day-to-day basis, environmental engineers conduct research, analyze scientific data, perform fieldwork, and prepare reports—all with the overall goal of safeguarding the environment.

Environmental engineers work for engineering and consulting firms, laboratories, and government agencies.

Currently, 54,000 environmental engineers are working in the United States. Job opportunities are expected to grow 25 percent by 2016 and, according to the U.S. Bureau of Labor Statistics (BLS), environmental engineers should be less affected by economic conditions than other sectors of the engineering profession.

A bachelor's degree in engineering, natural science, math, or a related field is essential for a career in environmental engineering. Some employers require a master's degree in engineering or a related field.

All 50 states and the District of Columbia require engineers who offer their services to the public to be licensed professional engineers (PEs). To obtain a license, environmental engineers must hold a bachelor's degree, have four years of relevant work experience, and complete a state exam. Recent graduates can get the licensing process underway by taking the exam in two stages. After successful completion of the first stage, Fundamentals of Engineering, they become Engineers in Training (EIT). The EIT designation is sufficient until environmental engineers have enough experience to take the second exam, Principles and Practices of Engineering, to earn the PE license.

The American Academy of Environmental Engineers (www.aaee.net) provides certification as Board Certified Environmental Engineer (BCEE) or Board Certified Member (BCM). The certifications require comprehensive written and oral exams in one or more areas of specialization, including general environmental engineering, air pollution control, hazardous waste management, wastewater engineering, and radiation protection. The certifications require a bachelor's degree, at least eight years of relevant experience, a PE license (for BCEE applicants), passing grades on written and oral exams, and ongoing professional education.

Environmental engineers earn a median annual wage of $69,940.

Water Resources Engineer

Water resources engineers are responsible for preparing water usage analyses; conducting flood hazard assessments; and conducting evaluations of groundwater management, water distribution, and sewage collection.

Often, water resources engineers also oversee the development and implementation of water conservation programs. To this end, they might develop resources and provide training to public utilities, government agencies, businesses, educational institutions, and the public.

During the course of their work, water resources engineers prepare technical memos and reports; write reports; and present their findings to other agencies, public utilities, and the public.

Inside Scoop
The World Wildlife Fund estimates that by 2025, two-thirds of the world's population could be facing serious water availability problems. Currently, the United States leads the world in per capita water consumption.

Water resource engineers need a minimum of a bachelor's degree in civil engineering, environmental science, biological resources engineering, or a related field. Most jobs require a master's degree and a PE license.

Several professional associations offer conferences, networking opportunities, and job listings for water resources engineers. These include the American Water Resources Association (www.awra.org), the Water Environment Federation (www.wef.org), and the American Water Works Association (www.awwa.org). The Environmental & Water Resources Institute (www.ewrinstitute.org) is a professional association that offers workshops in Water Infrastructure Security Enhancements, a course that focuses on improving security at water and wastewater facilities and enhancing water quality monitoring.

The median salary for a water resources engineer is $66,260 per year.

Environmental Meteorologist

Environmental meteorologists research environmental issues such as air quality and pollution. The job entails conducting air quality assessments, developing emissions estimates, submitting air permit applications, and preparing greenhouse gas analyses and *air dispersion modeling*, with the goal of addressing air quality issues.

def•i•ni•tion

Air dispersion modeling is a mathematical simulation of how air pollutants disperse in the atmosphere. These simulations are used to estimate the concentration of air pollutants, like factory and vehicle exhaust. The results are important for managing air quality.

Environmental meteorologists also study the effects of temperature, humidity, heat, and wind on air pollutants and prepare environmental impact reports about their impact on air quality, ozone depletion, and global warming. They also use the data to analyze how well pollution control systems are working.

Engineering companies, consulting firms, industrial plants, public utilities, and government agencies hire environmental meteorologists. In this field, travel, overtime, and fieldwork are common.

A bachelor's degree in atmospheric or environmental science, meteorology, or a related field is necessary to become an environmental meteorologist, and some positions require a master's degree or a Ph.D.

The Indoor Air Quality Association (www.iaqa.org), the American Indoor Air Quality Council (www.iaqcouncil.org), and the Association of Energy Engineers (www. aeecenter.org) offer certifications for environmental meteorologists who want to specialize in indoor air quality. The American Meteorological Society (www.ametsoc.org) also offers certification as a consulting meteorologist.

The median annual salary for an environmental meteorologist is $77,150.

Greenhouse Gas Engineer

Greenhouse gas engineers gather data, perform calculations, and develop plans for greenhouse gas emissions reduction. The job requires conducting feasibility studies, preparing energy management plans, and performing financial analysis.

Greenhouse gas engineers work for engineering and consulting firms. Currently, 30 states have established greenhouse gas reduction targets or proposed legislation to require greenhouse gas reporting, which will create more opportunities for greenhouse gas engineers.

A bachelor's degree in engineering or a related field is necessary to work as a greenhouse gas engineer; a master's degree can improve career opportunities.

def•i•ni•tion

Greenhouse gas is made up of gasses such as carbon dioxide, methane, nitrous oxide, and ozone that are present in the atmosphere that contribute to global warming. The increased temperatures resulting from greenhouse gas alter weather patterns, which can lead to species extinction and cause coastal flooding.

The Greenhouse Gas Management Institute (www.ghginstitute.org) is in the process of developing a series of professional certifications for practitioners and project managers. The Greenhouse Gas Experts Network (www.ghgnetwork.org) offers networking opportunities for professionals in the field.

The median salary for a greenhouse gas engineer is $98,380 per year.

Water Regulatory Analyst

Water regulatory analysts are responsible for creating policies to regulate the use of water. Their job is to analyze the impact of proposed water and sewer operations, develop programs to reduce water use, recommend public utility options for water conservation, and evaluate regulatory issues.

The U.S. Environmental Protection Agency (EPA) created the Clean Water Act (www. epa.gov/watertrain/cwa) in 1972 in an effort to eliminate all sources of water pollution. The Act provides ongoing federal financial assistance for municipal sewage treatment plant construction and sets regulatory requirements to reduce pollution from municipalities and industries.

Water regulatory analysts also work to educate the public about the importance of water conservation and provide tips on how to use less water, often through the distribution of educational materials and appearances at public meetings and events.

The daily duties of a water regulatory analyst can include analyzing utility reports and financial records to collect data on water usage, performing compliance audits, and making recommendations for programs to conserve water.

Public utilities are the largest employers of water regulatory analysts, although engineering and consulting firms also offer opportunities in the field.

Water regulatory analysts need a bachelor's degree in environmental science, public policy, or a related field. A master's degree can improve job prospects.

The American Water Works Association (www.awwa.org) offers several certification and training programs that improve opportunities for water regulatory analysts, including Water 101: Partnership for Safe Water, and Water and Wastewater Leadership.

The Association of Metropolitan Water Agencies (www.amwa.net) offers breaking news, trend reports, and conferences on issues relating to water utilities. Members also lobby for water policy changes, including legislation that safeguards the environment.

The median annual salary for a water regulatory analyst is $53,586.

Refuse and Recycling

On average, Americans toss enough trash to fill 63,000 garbage and recycling trucks per day. The diapers, glass bottles, and food scraps that end up in landfills, recycling facilities, and compost centers require employees to ensure they're disposed of safely. Awareness of the environmental impact of trash has led to more stringent controls for its disposal and, in the process, created new careers in composting facilities and deconstruction sites. Workers in these fields are taking a lead role in ensuring that materials ranging from jam jars to doorjambs are being recycled and reused.

Waste Management Planner

Waste management planners oversee the design, construction, and operation of waste management facilities such as landfills, recycling plants, and composting sites. Their goal is to find the most effective means to reduce, reuse, and recycle materials using the principles of *integrated solid waste management (ISWM)*.

Waste management planners are responsible for all aspects of waste management, from coordinating the collection and transportation of materials and consulting with communities to help them minimize and manage waste to designing landfills and ensuring materials are disposed of properly. To accomplish these goals, waste management planners apply the principles of sanitary design and waste-to-energy incineration. They also take into account city, state, and federal laws, as well as regulatory issues.

def•i•ni•tion

Integrated solid waste management (ISWM) refers to the process of minimizing the amount of waste that ends up in the landfill through waste prevention, composting, and recycling with minimal impact on the environment.

Waste management planners work for engineering and consulting firms, private companies, and government agencies. The educational requirements to enter the field vary widely. Some employers require a high school diploma, whereas others look for candidates with a bachelor's degree in environmental science or a related field.

WERC (www.werc.net), a consortium that focuses on environmental training for waste management professionals (including the legal aspects of environmental and natural resource management and the transportation of hazardous materials), offers continuing education programs and conferences.

Warning

Last year, there were 88 fatalities among waste management workers. Although the numbers have declined over the past decade (there were 109 deaths in 2003, according to the BLS), it's a field that demands extreme caution on the job.

The Solid Waste Association of North America (www.swana.org) and the National Solid Wastes Management Association (www.nswma.org) allow members to network with other waste management planners, access job postings, and read the latest news in the field of waste management.

The average annual salary for a waste management planner is $91,754.

Landfill and Recycling Center Supervisors

Landfill and recycling center supervisors oversee the operations for landfills and recycling centers. Their jobs involve accepting delivery of waste and recyclables, streamlining the collection process, developing policies and procedures, ensuring compliance with safety regulations, and following environmental policies.

Landfill and recycling center supervisors also review soil reports and provide data to environmental services staff, supervise required environmental testing, monitor and control all liquid and gas extraction systems, and conduct site audits. They also manage site budgets and hire and train staff—often following union guidelines.

> ### Inside Scoop
>
> Americans generate 251 million tons of waste every day, according to the U.S. Environmental Protection Agency (EPA). Currently, 32.5 percent of waste is recycled or composted, 12.5 percent is burned, and the remaining 55 percent goes to landfills.

A high school diploma is the minimum requirement to secure a job as a landfill and recycling center supervisor; some positions can require a bachelor's degree in environmental science or a related field. Knowledge of Occupational Safety and Health Administration (OSHA) principles is essential.

Joining the Solid Waste Association of North America (www.swana.org) and the National Solid Wastes Management Association (www.nswma.org) can provide insight into the field and access to job listings.

The median annual salary for a landfill and recycling center supervisor is $51,402.

Compost Center Supervisor

Compost center supervisors oversee the day-to-day operations of municipal or commercial composting centers. The job entails accepting materials from curbside and drop-off programs, conducting chemical analyses of the mixtures, monitoring the grinding of waste, and screening of the finished compost. On a daily basis, compost center supervisors measure carbon, nitrogen, moisture, and oxygen levels; use computer-based programs to develop recipes to aid in the breakdown of compost; and assess infrastructure needs to ensure optimal compost center operations.

A high school diploma is required to become a compost center supervisor. The U.S. Composting Council (www.compostingcouncil.org) offers continuing education courses to obtain specialized knowledge in the field.

The median wage for a compost center supervisor is $12 per hour.

def•i•ni•tion

Compost is a nutrient-rich soil substance created when organic waste, like food scraps and grass clippings, decompose. Decomposition speeds up when microorganisms such as bacteria and fungi are added to the compost.

Deconstruction Worker

Deconstruction workers break down houses, office buildings, barns, churches, factories, and other buildings piece by piece, saving the building materials to be recycled or reused.

Deconstruction workers use hammers, crowbars, crosscut saws, and other tools to remove building materials ranging from kitchen cabinets and molding to windows and doors. After the materials are removed, deconstruction workers might be required to clean up the construction site or deliver materials to building centers or recycling facilities.

Growing concern for reducing construction waste, combined with an increasing demand for recycled and salvaged building materials, has created more opportunities for deconstruction workers.

Inside Scoop

Unlike demolition—which emphasizes tearing down buildings as quickly and inexpensively as possible—deconstruction is a low-tech, labor-intensive process that focuses on salvaging materials. Deconstruction minimizes waste and conserves resources.

Inside Scoop

The Institute for Local Self-Reliance (www.ilsr.org) estimates that more than 200,000 jobs would be created across the United States if deconstruction were put into widespread use.

Deconstruction workers are often employed by non-profit organizations and home improvement centers specializing in salvaged materials.

A high school diploma or GED is required to secure a job as a deconstruction worker.

The median wage for deconstruction workers is $12 per hour.

Hazardous Materials Cleanup

Hazardous materials are not good for the environment. Asbestos, lead, arsenic, mold, and other hazardous substances pollute the water, air, and soil; harm wildlife; and have significant impacts on human health. Minimizing the use of hazardous materials is essential, but in cases where these substances still exist, workers are needed to remove, clean, transport, and store them safely. Increased awareness of the environmental impact of hazardous materials has created a wealth of opportunities in the field.

Asbestos and Lead Abatement Workers

Asbestos and lead abatement workers identify, remove, package, transport, and dispose of asbestos and lead. The job requires using tools such as vacuums, sandblasters, scrapers, and high-pressure sprayers to remove lead and asbestos.

During the removal process, asbestos and lead abatement workers (also called *remediation* or *decontamination workers*) continually monitor the amount of lead and asbestos in the air to minimize health and environmental hazards. They also use monitoring devices to identify the amount of asbestos and lead that needs to be removed.

Warning

Significant health hazards are associated with lead and asbestos. Asbestos, which was used to fireproof building materials like roofing and flooring, has been linked to lung cancer. Lead was a component of paint, pipes, and plumbing fixtures until the late 1970s and has been shown to cause hearing loss, seizures, hypertension, miscarriage, and other serious health effects. To safeguard their health, asbestos and lead abatement workers wear disposable coveralls, gloves, hardhats, shoe covers, safety glasses, chemical-resistant clothing, and face shields. Most workers also wear respirators while working to protect them from airborne particles or noxious gases.

Asbestos and lead abatement workers work for construction firms, waste management companies, and nuclear and electric plants. Overtime and shift work are common, especially when workers are required to respond to emergencies.

There are only 1,900 asbestos and lead abatement workers in the United States, according to the BLS. Job growth is expected to be strong in this field as a result of increased government regulations that require the removal of hazardous materials such as lead and asbestos to prevent further contamination of natural resources.

A high school diploma or GED is required to work as an asbestos and lead abatement worker. The government also requires workers to complete an OSHA-certified training program for the safe removal of asbestos and lead.

The median hourly wage for an asbestos and lead abatement worker is $16.75.

Decommissioning and Decontamination Worker

Decommissioning and decontamination workers remove and dispose of radioactive materials generated by nuclear facilities and power plants.

The job often requires working in cramped conditions to dismantle contaminated objects and remove radioactive material that has accumulated inside pipes and heat exchangers, which often involves using chemical, electrical, and ultrasonic processes. After the radioactive material is removed, decommissioning and decontamination workers are responsible for packaging it and shipping it to a disposal site.

The BLS predicts that opportunities for decommissioning and decontamination workers will increase significantly in response to increased demand for safer and cleaner nuclear facilities and power plants.

> **Inside Scoop**
>
> More than 70 test, demonstration, and power reactors have been retired in the United States since 1960.

A high school diploma or GED is required to secure a job as a decommissioning and decontamination worker. Working at nuclear facilities requires extensive and ongoing training, including a 40-hour training course in hazardous waste removal. Workers must pass classes mandated by the U.S. Nuclear Regulatory Commission (www.nrc.gov) that highlight regulations governing nuclear materials and radiation safety.

The Nuclear Energy Institute (www.nei.org) provides educational resources, news, and career information for professionals in the field.

The median wage for decommissioning and decontamination workers is $17.04 per hour.

Mold Specialist

Mold specialists remove mold from homes, office buildings, schools, factories, and other structures. During an initial consultation, mold specialists identify the presence of mold, assess the extent of the damage, and develop a plan for mold removal.

Mold specialists sand areas where mold is growing, remove damaged materials, and dispose of the hazardous waste following U.S. EPA safety guidelines. After mold is removed, mold specialists apply mold-inhibiting chemicals to prevent regrowth and, if necessary, replace contaminated building materials.

> **Inside Scoop**
>
> Mold can trigger health problems such as sinus congestion, coughing, asthma, sore throat, eye irritation, and respiratory infections.

The job often requires working in cramped spaces to remove mold from heating and air-conditioning ducts, behind walls, and in attics. During the removal process, mold specialists take special precautions—sealing off rooms and wearing protective coveralls, goggles, and respirators—to safeguard against health and environmental contamination.

The best opportunities for mold specialists are in the southeast United States and parts of the northeast and the northwest, where mold thrives.

Mold specialists need a high school diploma or GED. Advanced certifications like Certified Mold Inspector, Certified Mold Assessor, and Certified Mold Remediator offered by the National Association of Remediators and Mold Inspectors (www.normi.org), or Professional Mold Inspection Certification from the International Indoor Air Quality Commission (www.iiaqc.org) improve job prospects for mold specialists.

The median wage for a mold specialist is $16.75 per hour.

Hazardous Materials Containment and Removal Worker

Hazardous materials containment and removal workers are responsible for the treatment, storage, disposal, and transport of hazardous materials such as arsenic, mercury, lead, and asbestos. In doing their jobs, hazardous materials and containment workers follow local, state, and federal laws, including those set forth by the U.S. EPA and OSHA.

Hazardous materials containment and removal workers, also called *HAZMAT workers*, are employed at incinerator facilities, landfills, and private companies. Regardless of where they're employed, HAZMAT workers must follow strict procedures for the processing and storage of hazardous materials and keep accurate records on its transport and storage.

Inside Scoop

A federal program called Superfund (www.epa.gov/superfund) was created in 1980 to help clean up hazardous waste sites across the nation. The program was designed to ensure that hazardous waste sites are identified and tested with the goal of ensuring that all hazardous waste that was abandoned, accidentally spilled, or illegally dumped is cleaned up.

HAZMAT workers are often called on to respond to emergencies like a spill after a train derailment or a chemical weapons attack.

To do their jobs, HAZMAT workers must operate heavy machinery such as forklifts, earthmovers, and large trucks. Other equipment, like high-pressure cleaning equipment and remote devices, allow HAZMAT workers to locate and evaluate hazardous materials and package them for transportation or disposal.

The threat of contamination is high in this field. For this reason, it's essential for HAZMAT workers to wear coveralls, gloves, safety glasses, and shoe covers.

Overtime and shift work are common for hazardous materials containment and removal workers, especially for those specializing in disaster response.

Currently, there are 39,000 HAZMAT workers in the United States. Although numerous Superfund sites still require cleanup, the BLS predicts that declining federal funding could affect the number of hazardous materials containment and removal workers hired to clean up Superfund sites.

The median wage for a hazardous materials containment and removal worker is $17.04 per hour.

Chapter 8

Facilities Management

In This Chapter

- ♦ The green revolution taking place in facilities management careers
- ♦ Sharp increases in jobs for grounds maintenance workers
- ♦ Which jobs can help earn credits toward LEED certification
- ♦ Outlines of the qualifications necessary to land a job as an energy ret-rofitter or home performance technician

Hospitals, schools, factories, office buildings, and apartment complexes have one thing in common: the need for comprehensive facilities management. "Greening" facilities can take a number of forms. Turf grass managers might install efficient irrigation systems, facilities managers may switch to nontoxic cleaners, and HVAC technicians might recommend energy-efficient retrofits to heating and cooling equipment. These types of eco-friendly changes have positive impacts on the environment as well as the people who live and work in the facilities.

Job opportunities are declining in some areas of facilities management, but the jobs that remain offer significant opportunities to safeguard the environment while working 9-to-5.

Site Upkeep

Maintaining the landscapes of industrial complexes, apartment buildings, businesses, and office buildings takes the work of dedicated teams. Ensuring that the sites are maintained with the least impact on the environment requires extra effort and know-how—and employment opportunities for workers familiar with green landscaping techniques are growing.

Turf grass managers and grounds maintenance workers are on the front lines of grounds management, taking a lead role in applying nontoxic fertilizers, using efficient irrigation systems, and employing nonmotorized tools.

Turf Grass Manager

Working as a turf grass manager involves overseeing the care and maintenance of large grassy areas in places such as sod farms, playing fields, and golf courses. Turf grass managers are responsible for the upkeep of the turf, including seeding, aeration, weeding, and fertilizing. They also oversee the installation, maintenance, and repair of irrigation systems. In stadiums and on playing fields, turf grass managers are also in charge of drawing markings on the turf, setting up sports equipment, and taking care of special events needs such as stages and additional seating.

In an effort to promote eco-friendly turf grass management, the job might entail recommending nonchemical fertilizers, using native grass seed, and researching water-saving irrigation systems.

A high school diploma or GED is the minimum educational requirement for turf grass managers. Many also have bachelor's degrees and certification by the Professional Grounds Management Society (PGMS) to aid in their understanding of turf grass physiology, botany, and plant diseases.

Turf grass managers earn an average of $35,340 per year.

Grounds Maintenance Worker

Grounds maintenance workers are responsible for the upkeep of the grounds at parks, public buildings, and housing projects. Their role is to care for the grass, trees, shrubs, and flowers, performing tasks like planting, mowing, pruning, and weeding.

The focus on environmentally friendly landscape design often requires grounds maintenance workers to plant native species, use natural fertilizers and nontoxic pesticides and herbicides, and compost yard waste. Grounds maintenance workers can safeguard the environment by using mulching mowers and removing weeds using hand tools and rakes instead of leaf blowers—especially on smaller jobs.

Grounds maintenance workers can help earn credits toward Leadership in Energy and Environmental Design (LEED) certification by implementing plans for integrated pest management, erosion control, stormwater management, and water-efficient landscaping.

> **Inside Scoop**
>
> Yard waste, such as grass clippings, makes up 20 percent of municipal solid waste, with the majority going to landfills.

Grounds maintenance workers work outdoors and might have to endure extreme temperatures. The job often requires traveling from one site to another, especially if the worker is employed by a landscaping business that provides services to a number of clients. The work is often seasonal in nature, with the highest number of jobs available from March through October.

> **Inside Scoop**
>
> States with the highest concentrations of grounds maintenance workers are Idaho, Arizona, Hawaii, South Carolina, and Nevada. The top-paying states for grounds maintenance workers are Connecticut; Rhode Island; Delaware; New York; and Washington, D.C.

Grounds maintenance workers must be physically fit, must be able to lift up to 50 pounds, and might be required to have a valid driver's license. No formal education is required for grounds maintenance workers, although several community colleges offer certifications in grounds maintenance.

The PGMS (www.pgms.org) also offers ongoing professional development programs, including Certified Grounds Manager and Certified Grounds Technician programs. PGMS also presents annual Green Star awards to workers who contribute to the aesthetics and maintenance of a landscape.

According to the U.S. Bureau of Labor Statistics (BLS), job opportunities for grounds maintenance workers are expected to grow by 18 percent, creating upwards of 270,000 new jobs, by 2016, largely due to the increase in construction and parkland. Currently, more than 1.5 million people are employed as grounds maintenance workers in the United States.

The average wage for a grounds maintenance worker is $10.30 per hour; supervisors earn an average of $35,340 per year.

Installation and Maintenance

To meet the goals of green building, the commitment to safeguarding the environment needs to be extended long after construction is complete.

Installation and maintenance workers are on the front lines when it comes to installing energy-efficient mechanical, electrical, and plumbing systems and keeping them properly maintained.

In addition to overseeing the overall operation of industrial, commercial, educational, and residential facilities, installation and maintenance workers manage the day-to-day operations and take lead roles in ensuring that the health of the planet is a priority by maintaining equipment to operate at peak performance, spearheading recycling programs, and using nontoxic products.

Facilities Manager

Facilities managers oversee the management of buildings, grounds, equipment, supplies, and staff for government and educational institutions, industrial complexes, parks and recreation departments, shopping malls, apartment buildings, and other facilities.

Facilities managers must have a thorough understanding of structures and their environments. Depending on the size and scale of the operation, facilities managers might engage in space planning, budgeting, purchasing and selling real estate, managing facility operations, and integrating technology for interior and exterior spaces.

Establishing guidelines for maintaining environmentally friendly facilities falls on the facilities manager. He must make decisions about purchasing green cleaning products, implementing nontoxic solutions for pest management, and reducing energy use. In some cases, facilities managers can even play roles in steering renovations and retrofits toward the use of greener energy alternatives such as solar panels.

Facilities managers are directly responsible for several credits necessary for LEED certification, including using sustainable cleaning products, materials, and equipment and purchasing materials made from renewable/recycled products.

The educational requirements for facilities managers vary widely depending on the organization. In some cases, extensive experience as facilities staff can result in a promotion to management. In other cases, experience and advanced education are required.

The International Facility Management Association (www.ifma.org) offers credentials as a Certified Facility Manager. The Association of Higher Education Facilities Officers (APPA) also offers certificates for facilities managers working in educational institutions. The APPA offers two programs—Educational Facilities Professional (EFP) and Certified Educational Facilities Professional (CEFP).

According to the BLS, the demand for facilities managers is expected to increase by 12 percent by 2016, in part due to the focus on maximizing the efficiency of facility operations. To this end, facilities managers with experience streamlining operations, improving profitability, and incorporating energy-saving programs will be the most sought after.

Facilities managers earn an average of $58,000 per year.

Energy Retrofitter

Energy retrofitters use technological solutions to enhance the efficiency of the energy systems in homes, businesses, and factories. Using reports created by energy auditors, energy retrofitters perform upgrades, or retrofits, to electrical and mechanical systems.

The duties of an energy retrofitter include installing energy-efficient HVAC systems, upgrading plumbing, and replacing windows with the overall goal of saving energy and reducing operating costs. The improvements made by energy retrofitters can help facilities and homeowners earn federal tax credits. Other responsibilities, such as assisting in the development and implementation of quality assurance procedures for energy projects, conducting site visits to verify the installation of energy equipment, and writing reports to summarize the results of a retrofit, might also be required of an energy retrofitter.

Energy retrofitters often have backgrounds in facilities, HVAC, or other trades. A college education in a related field, coupled with on-the-job training, is needed for a job as an energy retrofitter. Advanced certification is also available—and desirable. The National Energy Management Institute (www.nemionline.org) offers certification for energy retrofitters through its Testing, Adjusting, Balancing Bureau (TABB) in Indoor Air Quality and Commissioning. The Association of Energy Engineers also offers a Certified Energy Manager (CEM) certificate.

Due to the newness of the field, the BLS does not have statistics on average job growth among energy retrofitters. According to the Association of Energy Engineers (www.aeecenter.org), career opportunities are exploding. In the past year, attendance has increased 200 percent in classes for CEM certification with plenty of job opportunities awaiting graduates.

The median salary for an energy retrofitter is $37,440 per year.

Home Performance Technician

A home performance technician analyzes all the systems in a home to evaluate their efficiency and make recommendations for performance improvements.

Whereas energy retrofitters focus only on the energy systems in a home, home performance technicians examine all aspects of the home from stormwater management and water usage to insulation levels and indoor air quality.

Inside Scoop

The average homeowner spends $1,900 per year on energy costs. The high costs are due in part to the fact that more than half of the homes in the United States were built before modern energy codes and many have inadequate insulation, high levels of air infiltration, poor duct systems, and inefficient heating and air-conditioning systems.

After problems are identified, home performance technicians work with clients to implement solutions. Home performance technicians might install control devices on appliances to reduce energy and water use, add insulation, improve lighting systems, repair or replace flashing and downspouts on roofs, and service HVAC systems.

Most home performance technicians work for private companies that conduct assessments for residential customers. Some might work for state governments, utility companies, or trade organizations.

Home performance technicians can help earn credits toward LEED certification by installing, upgrading, or retrofitting plumbing, lighting, ventilation, energy, and stormwater management systems.

A growing number of states are participating in home performance programs, such as Home Performance with ENERGY STAR (www.energystar.gov), a national program from the U.S. Environmental Protection Agency (EPA) and the U.S. Department of Energy (DOE) that allows homeowners to take advantage of federal tax credits for improving energy efficiency. The increased demand for these programs has created a wealth of opportunities for home performance technicians.

Home performance technicians often have experience in other building trades, such as construction management, HVAC installation, or plumbing.

Several organizations, such as the Building Performance Institute (www.bpi.org) and North American Technician Excellence (www.natex.org), offer standardized guidelines and educational programs toward certification as a home performance technician. The AEE offers several certifications that are valuable for home performance technicians, including Certified Energy Manager, Certified Indoor Air Quality Professional, and Certified Lighting Efficiency Professional.

The average salary for a home performance technician is $46,250.

HVAC Technician

HVAC technicians are responsible for the installation, maintenance, and repair of heating, ventilation, and air-conditioning systems. Their work requires traveling to job sites and can involve working in residential, commercial, and industrial settings. Some HVAC technicians specialize in either installation or maintenance and repair but are trained to do both.

An HVAC technician can improve the energy usage of a building by installing energy-efficient heating and air-conditioning systems, attic ventilation systems, and solar fans or by retrofitting wood-burning fireplaces. New HVAC systems can also improve overall air quality.

Increased concern for the environment has led to the development of energy-saving heating and air-conditioning systems, creating more job opportunities for HVAC technicians. In addition to installing more energy-efficient systems, HVAC technicians are expected to have more opportunities because systems need to be maintained for peak efficiency. Also, new regulations prohibiting the discharge and production of certain refrigerants are expected to lead to the need to replace air-conditioning systems for upgraded models with environmentally safe refrigerants.

Several LEED certification credits can be affected by HVAC technicians, including the energy performance of building systems, increased ventilation, outdoor air delivery monitoring, and the controllability of systems. HVAC technicians can also opt to earn certification as LEED APs, increasing their job prospects and earning additional LEED credits. HVAC technicians who are LEED APs have a superior knowledge of LEED certification requirements, enabling them to make recommendations for HVAC components to earn LEED credits.

HVAC technicians travel to job sites and might be required to be on-call. The job often requires working outside and in cramped spaces. During peak seasons, HVAC technicians may work more than 40 hours per week.

Warning

Safety precautions are essential for HVAC technicians. On the job, they might be exposed to hazardous refrigerants that can cause skin damage, frostbite, or blindness, making it necessary to wear proper clothing and masks. HVAC technicians are also at risk for electrical shock and burns, so it's necessary to take precautions on the job.

HVAC technicians require advanced education to become proficient in the field. Colleges and trade schools offer programs ranging from six months to two years.

Apprenticeship programs are also commonplace. They combine paid on-the-job training with classroom instruction and typically last from three to five years. Certain states require licenses.

On average, HVAC technicians earn $18.11 per hour.

Chapter 9

Transportation

In This Chapter

- ◆ Government legislation that has paved the way for new careers in the transportation industry
- ◆ New training classes and certifications on the latest automotive and aerospace technologies
- ◆ The role transportation planners play in safeguarding the environment
- ◆ The impact of recyclable materials on mass transit design and maintenance

On any given day, millions of Americans play a role in their own version of *Planes, Trains, and Automobiles* as they drive, ride, or fly to destinations across town and around the world. Transportation is a mainstay of American culture; it is also one of the least environmentally friendly industries in the world. Currently, 67 percent of the 21 million barrels of oil used in the United States every day and one-third of greenhouse gas emissions are transportation-related.

Concern for the environmental impacts of all modes of transportation has led to the research and development of new technologies such as electric cars, hybrid buses, light rail, and hydrogen-powered airplanes—and to the creation of new jobs in this sector. Investments in fuel efficiency alone are expected to create an additional 241,000 new jobs by 2020, including 23,800 in the automotive sector, according to the Union of Concerned Scientists (www.ucsusa.org). So, let's buckle up and explore green careers in transportation.

Research and Development

Before hybrid cars started selling like hotcakes and light rail trains started welcoming passengers onboard, they were just concepts. New transportation technologies from electric engines to recyclable body panels all started out as ideas that needed to be researched and prototyped before they hit the market. Automakers, aerospace manufacturers, and government agencies invest billions of dollars in research and development. Right now, their focus is on improving fuel efficiency and lessening environmental impact, which has opened up a range of job opportunities.

Automotive Engineer

Automotive engineers design cars, trucks, SUVs, and motorcycles. Their jobs are to come up with original concepts, create blueprints, and follow their designs through the manufacturing process. To accomplish these goals, automotive engineers use a combination of mechanical, electrical, software, and electronic engineering principles.

During the design process, automotive engineers take into account government regulations for crash controls; vehicle dynamics such as handling, steering, and braking; durability, ergonomics engineering; drivability; and cost. Automotive engineers are also concerned with *fuel economy* and *emissions*.

def•i•ni•tion

Fuel economy measures how efficiently a vehicle converts fuel into useful performance. In the United States, fuel economy is calculated in miles per gallon.

Emissions are the measurement of hydrocarbons, nitrogen oxide, carbon monoxide, carbon dioxide, and evaporative emissions released by a car.

Automotive engineers are on the cutting edge of advances in automotive design. Innovations developed by automotive engineers are responsible for improving average fuel economy, creating zero-emissions vehicles, and using waste-based biofuels to power automobiles.

The surge in demand for eco-friendly vehicles has led to more opportunities for automotive engineers to design hybrids, plug-in hybrid electric vehicles, biodiesel, fuel cells, and multifuel vehicles. According to the U.S. Bureau of Labor Statistics (BLS), the demand for automotive engineers will increase 20 percent by 2016, creating 41,000 new jobs.

Inside Scoop

In 2007, Congress passed new legislation that requires automakers to make their new lines of cars, trucks, and SUVs capable of averaging 35 miles per gallon by 2020. The bill included provisions that would promote alternative fuels, including ethanol, and provide more grants and loan guarantees to makers of fuel-efficient vehicles. Automakers will look to automotive engineers to design more fuel-efficient vehicles as they strive to meet these requirements.

Automotive engineers require a minimum of a master's degree with a concentration in mechanical, electronic/electrical, or manufacturing engineering. Automakers like General Motors and Ford often require a Ph.D. for positions in research and development.

The Society of Automotive Engineers (www.sae.org) offers professional development classes, networking events, conferences, and job listings to its members.

The median salary for an automotive engineer is $68,620 per year.

Automobile Marketing Manager

Automobile marketing managers conduct market research; participate in product development; implement marketing strategies; oversee sales, advertising, and promotion; and coordinate public relations activities for all aspects of automobile sales.

The booming demand for environmentally friendly vehicles has led to new opportunities for marketing managers who understand all aspects of brand development and promotion. Marketing managers with experience launching new products and developing advertising and media relations campaigns—especially in the auto industry—will be in high demand. In fact, employment for marketing managers is expected to increase 12 percent by 2016, creating almost 70,000 new jobs.

In the automotive industry, marketing managers can work for automakers such as General Motors, Ford, Honda, and Toyota, dealerships, rental car agencies, or *car-sharing programs*.

def•i•ni•tion

A **car-sharing program** enables members to share a fleet of vehicles located throughout a community. Members can borrow cars for short periods of time, often by the hour, without any of the expenses of car ownership, such as maintenance and insurance. There are 18 car-sharing programs in the United States with 234,483 members—an increase of up to 75 percent since 2007.

Automotive marketing managers are responsible for designing media campaigns to promote alternative fuel and fuel-efficient vehicles, implementing sales incentive programs for eco-friendly autos, and developing materials about the environmental benefits of their vehicles to car buyers.

Marketing managers who work for auto dealerships might send out press releases and talk to the media about the green features of their dealerships, such as buildings certified by Leadership in Energy and Environmental Design (LEED), geothermal heating systems, or their practice of recycling car wash water. In rental car agencies and car-sharing programs, marketing managers take a lead role in promoting the availability of hybrid and fuel-efficient vehicles on a short-term basis.

Automotive marketing managers need a minimum of a bachelor's degree with a major in marketing or communications. Landing a job at a top automaker requires a master's degree in business administration (MBA) or a Ph.D. with an emphasis on marketing.

Membership in the American Association of Marketing (www.marketingpower.com) or the Public Relations Society of America (www.prsa.org) denotes a certain level of experience in the field. Both organizations also offer continuing education in marketing and public relations to help marketing managers build their skills or pursue areas of specialization.

Automobile dealers employ the largest number of marketing managers of all industries. According to BLS, marketing managers in the auto industry earn a median salary of $101,110 per year.

Quality Control Analyst

Quality control analysts take lead roles in monitoring quality standards for all the parts and materials that go into the production cycle of a vehicle. Using special measuring tools, instruments, and precision equipment, quality control analysts perform inspections, identify defects, and make repair recommendations.

Quality control analysts are employed in every sector of the manufacturing industry, from vehicle assembly to food production. In the transportation industry, quality control analysts work for automakers, aerospace manufacturers, or parts companies.

The advent of new transportation technologies, such as plug-in hybrid electric vehicles, fuel cells, and lightweight material alternatives designed to make vehicles and planes more environmentally friendly, has made it increasingly important for quality control analysts to be involved in product design, development, and production.

Career Crisis

The trend toward using self-monitoring production machines in the auto industry means that opportunities for quality control analysts are declining as the position becomes more automated. BLS estimates employment for quality control analysts will decline 7 percent by 2016. In fact, inspection duties are increasingly being distributed to fabrication and assembly workers, instead of being managed by quality control analysts.

In some companies, a high school diploma is the minimum requirement for a quality control analyst. To secure an upper-level position with opportunities for advancement, though, a bachelor's degree in engineering or manufacturing is highly recommended.

The International Organization for Standardization (www.iso.org) offers training programs in standardization and project management to help quality control analysts ensure the compatibility and interoperability of automotive products and increase distribution efficiency. The American Society for Quality (www.asq.org) offers training and certification on a range of quality control topics, including auditing automotive controls, quality management, and social responsibility.

The median wage for a quality control analyst is $16.74 per hour.

Aviation Designer

Aviation designers design, develop, and test aircraft from single-engine planes to jumbo jets. Some aviation designers (also called *aerospace engineers* or *aeronautical engineers*) specialize in a certain type of aircraft, such as commercial planes, military fighter jets, or helicopters; others are experts in a certain aspect of aviation design, such as aerodynamics, thermodynamics, acoustics, propulsion, or navigation. Their jobs involve structural design, navigation and control, instrumentation, and production.

A growing number of aviation designers are focusing on improving fuel efficiency and reducing pollution. The scope of this work ranges from reducing the weight of the plane and improving aerodynamics to designing systems that minimize noise pollution.

Aviation designers at Boeing (www.boeing.com) deem green planes a research priority. They are working on developing low-noise planes and using biofuels and hydrogen to power aircraft. They are also exploring environmentally friendly propulsion alternatives.

There are 90,000 aviation designers in the United States, according to BLS. Most work for major airlines or aerospace corporations such as Lockheed Martin (www.lockheedmartin.com) and Boeing. Approximately 12 percent work for government agencies like the U.S. Department of Defense, the U.S. Department of Transportation, and the National Aeronautics and Space Administration. Three percent are self-employed—many as consultants.

Career Crisis

A perceived lack of opportunities in the field of aviation design has resulted in fewer students applying to accredited programs. According to BLS, by 2016, there will not be enough new graduates to replace outgoing aviation designers.

The Aerospace Industries Association (www.aia-aerospace.org) reports that 60 percent of the aerospace workforce in the United States is 45 or older, noting that it's a good time to pursue an education in this.

A bachelor's degree in aerospace or aeronautical engineering is essential, although few positions are available to job seekers without at least a master's degree. A Ph.D. in aerospace engineering or mechanical engineering is highly recommended. In most cases, aviation designers need to pass extensive background checks to obtain high-level security clearance.

Membership in the American Institute of Aeronautics and Astronautics (www.aiaa.org) can provide job leads, networking opportunities, and access to industry events.

Aviation designers earn a median salary of $87,610 per year.

Repair and Maintenance

It's not enough to design and develop green transportation alternatives. After the latest eco-friendly options hit the streets, hybrid/fuel cell/biodiesel/hydrogen cars, trucks, SUVs, and airplanes—and all their green components—will need qualified professionals to repair and maintain them. Right now, the BLS estimates that the demand for qualified auto and aviation mechanics far exceeds the availability of trained workers. The demand is especially strong for workers who are trained in the latest technologies. In other words, mechanics who are trained on the Toyota Prius and not the Dodge Dart will have plenty of job opportunities.

Auto Mechanic

Auto mechanics inspect, maintain, and repair cars, light trucks, SUVs, and motorcycles. The job has evolved from performing simple mechanical repairs into a highly technical craft, requiring auto mechanics to keep abreast of the latest automotive technologies.

In the past, mechanics worked only on gas-powered vehicles. The surge in the number of hybrid and alternative-fuel vehicles, including ones that use biodiesel or ethanol, has created a demand for auto mechanics with advanced knowledge of fuel-efficient vehicles.

> **Inside Scoop**
>
> More than 345,000 hybrid vehicles were sold in 2007—an increase of 35 percent over the previous year. The growing demand is good news for auto mechanics who specialize in green vehicles because new hybrid owners need people to maintain their cars.

By properly disposing of airbags, paint, and tires and recycling motor oil and antifreeze, auto mechanics can play a significant role in reducing the environmental impact of their jobs.

Rapid changes in automotive technology have increased the demand for trained auto mechanics. According to the BLS, more than 110,000 new jobs will become available for auto mechanics over the next decade, increasing the overall demand by 14 percent.

The best opportunities are available to auto mechanics who have training from vocational schools or community colleges. In addition to teaching the basics of auto mechanics, such as diagnostics and repair, most programs have started offering specific classes about hybrid and alternative-fuel vehicles.

Auto mechanics who graduated before the advent of these types of vehicles can upgrade their skills through continuing education courses. Organizations like the Automotive Service Association (www.asashop.org) offer ongoing training in the latest technologies. Automobile manufacturers also offer training on their specific brands. Toyota, for example, sponsors the Toyota Technical Education Network (www.toyota.com/about/tten) at colleges and vocational schools across the country.

Auto mechanics can find work at car and truck dealerships, garages, service stations, and franchises. They earn a median hourly wage of $16.24.

Auto Retrofitter

Auto retrofitters make adjustments to specific automotive systems to improve their performance. In the past, auto retrofitters were focused on tweaking the mechanical systems to make cars faster. Now, the growing demand for cars that pollute less and are more efficient has led to new opportunities for auto retrofitters.

Most auto retrofitters are skilled mechanics who specialize in performance-enhancing repairs, such as changing a diesel engine to run on biodiesel, converting from gas to electric power, or using more environmentally friendly refrigerants in vehicle air conditioners. Auto retrofitters can also focus on services to improve fuel efficiency and decrease emissions.

Inside Scoop

The demand for improved fuel efficiency and decreased emissions has created a new market for specialty automotive products. The automotive aftermarket, which includes sales of replacement parts, accessories, lubricants, tools, and specialty equipment, is a $34.3 billion industry that employs 4.5 million people. Auto retrofitters have contributed to the growth of the specialty auto equipment industry by purchasing parts and equipment to improve the environmental performance of the vehicles they service.

Auto retrofitters are trained auto mechanics with additional training in performance enhancements. In addition to completing a program in auto mechanics from a community college or vocational school, advanced certifications can improve job opportunities. Automotive Training Centres (www.autotrainingcentre.com) offers courses in ozone depletion and air-conditioning retrofits. In addition, The National Institute for Automotive Service Excellence (www.ase.com) offers classes in refrigerant recovery and recycling.

Like auto mechanics, auto retrofitters can work at car and truck dealerships, garages, service stations, and franchises. The BLS estimates that 16 percent are self-employed. The median salary is $16.24 per hour.

Aviation Mechanic

Aviation mechanics perform the same duties as auto mechanics—inspection, maintenance, and repair—but specialize in aircraft, not automobiles. Known as *airframe mechanics* or *avionics technicians*, they are concerned with preventive maintenance, performing scheduled checks based on the number of hours a plane has flown and/or the date of last inspection. Their jobs can include inspecting aircraft engines, landing gear, and instruments and performing necessary repair or replacement of parts. Other job duties for aviation mechanics include checking for corrosion and cracks in the fuselage, wings, and tail and repairing sheet metal or composite surfaces.

Aviation mechanics also complete inspections required by the Federal Aviation Administration (FAA; www.faa.gov) and are required to keep detailed records on all maintenance performed on the aircraft. Regardless of the type of work an aviation mechanic is performing, her goal is to work quickly to put the aircraft back into service as soon as possible.

Some aviation mechanics work on one specific type of aircraft, such as jets. Others specialize in one certain aviation system, such as engines or hydraulics.

The emphasis on designing new fleets of aircraft that are made from lightweight composite materials, like graphite and fiberglass, and are powered by alternative fuels and solar power require aviation mechanics to understand and be able to work on environmentally friendly systems. To this end, schools are placing emphasis on integrating lessons on up-and-coming green technologies into their curriculums. Often, aviation mechanics gain experience in these systems on the job, working on the latest environmentally friendly innovations as they become available.

Inside Scoop

A flight from New York to Denver generates between 840 and 1,660 pounds of carbon dioxide per passenger—about the same amount that an SUV generates in a month. By 2050, aircraft emissions are expected to be one of the largest contributors to global warming. Developing greener aircraft can significantly reduce the environmental impact of aviation. An increase in the demand for more eco-friendly aircraft and flight systems is creating greater need for aviation mechanics who want to use their knowledge of airplane mechanics to work on greener aircraft.

Aviation mechanics often work in hangars, but it's also common for work to be performed outdoors if an aircraft needs immediate repairs. It's essential for aviation mechanics to work well under pressure because of the time-sensitive nature of their work. The job requires the ability to lift up to 70 pounds and work in awkward positions to access engines and control systems. Most aviation mechanics work 40 hours per week on 8-hour shifts that run around the clock; overtime and weekend work is common.

FAA-certified training is recommended for the best job opportunities. One hundred seventy trade schools are certified by the FAA in the United States, offering two- and four-year degrees in avionics, aviation technology, and aviation maintenance. FAA regulations require students to log a minimum of 1,900 class hours to earn certification.

In some cases, aviation mechanics in the Armed Forces acquire enough experience to satisfy the work experience requirements for the FAA certificate.

Aviation mechanics must pass an exam for certification and take at least 16 hours of training every 24 months to keep their certificates current. Some aviation mechanic jobs require additional licenses, such as a radiotelephone license issued by the U.S. Federal Communications Commission (www.fcc.gov).

Career Crisis

Fewer students are entering technical schools to learn trades like aviation mechanics. According to the BLS, students with the aptitude to pursue careers in airplane maintenance and repair are choosing to enter other technical fields, such as computer science. As a result, the supply of trained aviation mechanics is not keeping pace with the demand for their skills.

Approximately 138,000 aviation mechanics are working in the United States. They work for major airlines, aircraft manufacturers, companies with private planes, and the federal government. Competition is fierce for jobs with major airlines because of the above-average pay and benefits.

There is room to advance in the field. With enough experience, aviation mechanics can be promoted to lead mechanic, shop supervisor, or lead inspector. Aviation mechanics can also pursue work as inspectors with the FAA.

Approximately 30 percent of aviation mechanics are members of unions such as the International Association of Machinists and Aerospace Workers and the Transport Workers Union of America.

Aviation mechanics earn a median wage of $22.95 per hour.

Mass Transit

Mass transit is one of the most environmentally friendly transportation options. Riding the bus or taking the train instead of driving saves energy and reduces greenhouse gas emissions.

Improving access to mass transit by adding new bus routes and expanding rail and streetcar service is part of the solution—one that is being promoted by government initiatives. In 2007, Congress passed a bill allocating $1.9 billion per year for six years to expand passenger rail lines in the United States. Using eco-friendly materials and manufacturing processes to support mass transit initiatives is also essential. Trained workers are needed to help achieve these goals, making it a good time to think about becoming a train operator, transportation planner, or construction manager.

Transportation Planner

Transportation planners, as the title suggests, handle all aspects of transportation planning including research, design, maintenance, construction, and operations for all modes of transportation including roads, bridges, railroads, and airports.

Transportation planners take into account existing infrastructure, land use regulations, environmental factors, and passenger needs. These jobs can involve preparing detailed budgets, hiring contractors, acting as a liaison with architects and engineers, and participating in public meetings to answer questions about transportation projects.

Some transportation planners specialize in one specific mode of transportation like highway planning, railroad planning, or airport planning. Highway planners oversee the planning, design, and construction of highways and roads, including bicycle and pedestrian paths. Railroad planners are responsible for mass transit systems, including the design and construction of light rails and monorails and station location and aesthetics. Airport planners design and construct airports. They take into account the needs of aircraft to create blueprints for airport facilities and analyze predominant wind directions to determine runway orientation.

One of the newest specializations is bicycle transportation planning. As the demand for eco-friendly modes of transportation grows, so does the demand for planners to oversee the design and construction of bicycle lanes and related facilities, such as bicycle racks on trains and buses.

Transportation engineers play a role in safeguarding the environment by conserving historic roads; implementing and promoting green modes of transportation such as public transit and bicycle and pedestrian paths; and designing roads to protect nature reserves, parks, and wetlands.

Transportation planners need a minimum of a bachelor's degree in civil engineering or urban planning. A master's degree in civil engineering or a related field is preferred. The Institute of Transportation Engineers (www.ite.org) offers additional certifications including Professional Traffic Operations Engineer, Professional Transportation Planner, Traffic Operations Practitioner Specialist, and Traffic Signal Operations Specialist that can improve job opportunities.

Congress is reviewing the Green Transportation Infrastructure Research and Technology Transfer Act, which, if passed, will provide grants to carry out green transportation infrastructure research and development. The goal of the bill is to preserve and restore floodplains and wetlands, recharge natural aquifers, manage stormwater using natural methods, and minimize energy consumption and land pollution. If the bill passes, it will create new green-collar jobs in the transportation industry, including jobs for transportation planners.

A growing population has spurred the need to upgrade existing infrastructure and has increased demand for transportation planners. The BLS estimates that job opportunities in this field will increase 18 percent by 2016, with a specific emphasis on transportation planners who can design and construct infrastructure that preserves the environment and meets the growing demand for eco-friendly transportation options.

Most transportation planners work for engineering firms or government agencies. However, a small percentage of transportation planners are self-employed as consultants.

The median salary for a transportation planner is $68,600 per year.

Mass Transit Construction Manager

Construction managers on mass transit projects oversee all aspects of planning, design, site preparation, and construction of mass transit projects such as light rail lines and streetcar tracks. Their jobs include creating budgets and timelines, handling contract administration, adhering to local bylaws, hiring subcontractors, coordinating inspections, and providing general project oversight. Their work is often done in conjunction with the Federal Transit Administration (www.fta. dot.gov).

Construction managers on mass transit projects can choose materials like railroad ties made of recycled plastic, install digitally controlled train crossing signals, and use alternative power sources to lessen the environmental impact of their work.

Demand for mass transit systems has spiked, leading to more jobs in all areas of mass transit. The United States House of Representatives recently passed a bill appropriating $1.7 billion for mass transit system investment, which will create a wealth of new jobs in public transportation.

Construction managers might work on upgrading or extending existing infrastructure or oversee the construction of new light rail lines, streetcar tracks, and transit stations.

A bachelor's degree in construction management, civil engineering, or a related field improves job prospects for construction managers. Securing a position with a government agency or overseeing a large project likely requires a master's degree in a discipline such as construction science.

Additional certifications are also helpful. The National Transit Institute (www.ntionline.com) offers programs in managing the environmental review process. The American Institute of Constructors (www.aicnet.org) and the Construction Management Association of America (www.cmaanet.org) also offer general certificates in construction management.

Construction managers working on mass transit projects can work for engineering firms or government agencies.

The median salary for a construction manager is $75,200.

Bus Driver and Train Operator

Bus drivers and train operators transport passengers along various transportation routes through cities, states, and countries. Their routes might be short—a single loop through a metropolitan area—or long—a multiweek chartered excursion.

At first glance, mass transit operation might not seem like a green career, but advances in transportation technology have turned these occupations into hot green-collar jobs.

In cities across the United States, bus drivers are fueling up with biodiesel or driving hybrid buses and train operators are operating electric-powered streetcars or light rail trains. In an effort to further green mass transit, some bus drivers are minimizing idling to reduce pollution and keeping heating and cooling systems running at moderate temperatures to conserve energy.

Bus drivers and train operators drive set routes, collect fares, issue transfers, and answer passenger questions about schedules and routes.

Bus drivers and train operators need a high school diploma or GED and must meet the qualifications established by state and federal governments,

> **Inside Scoop**
>
> Last year, more than 10 billion trips were taken on public transportation—the highest ridership in 49 years—turning public transportation into a $44 billion industry that employs more than 360,000 people.

which include a commercial driver's license. Drug testing and background checks are required by some employers.

Inside Scoop

According to the American Public Transportation Association (www.apta.com), those closest to public transportation drive an average 4,400 fewer miles a year than those whose homes are not located near bus or rail lines. This reduces annual carbon emissions in the United States by 37 million metric tons per year, which is equal to the electric power used by 4.9 million households.

Most bus drivers and train operators work for government agencies such as transit authorities, although jobs are also available with private companies offering long-haul routes and chartered excursions. There are 653,000 bus drivers and 125,000 rail transportation workers in the United States. The job outlook is strong for both, according to the BLS, with anticipated growth of 10 percent by 2016.

Bus drivers earn a median hourly wage of $15.43, subway and streetcar operators earn a median wage of $23.55 per hour, and rail transportation employees (including train operators) earn a median wage of $27.88 per hour.

Metal Fabricator

Metal fabricators create the machines that form metal into products such as light rail tracks, transit shelters, and bike racks for buses and trains. The job involves using specialized drills, grinders, molds, presses, and rollers to machine, form, and powder-coat metal.

Metal fabricators are responsible for creating all the metal parts necessary for production and assembly. Technology has made the job more complex, requiring metal fabricators to program machines and perform minor repairs instead of just operating machinery.

Environmental concerns about metal have led a growing number of metal fabricators to start working with aluminum. Aluminum is a more sustainable metal that can be used in a variety of mass transit applications, including reflective roofing on transit shelters and lighting grids in subways. Metal fabricators can also lessen their environmental impact by recycling scrap materials that can be melted down and reused.

Career Crisis

High-tech production techniques, such as employing robots, computers, and programmable equipment, have increased productivity but decreased opportunities for metal fabricators. In fact, the BLS projects a 12 percent decrease in jobs for metalworkers by 2016.

High gas prices and concerns about pollution have led to a growing demand for mass transit options. Over the past decade, capital investments for bus and rail lines have increased up to 28 percent. Although the demand for metal fabricators is declining overall, the need for more streetcar, light rail, and commuter rail tracks should provide new jobs on mass transit projects.

Most metal fabricators work for private companies in small shops that have fewer than 20 employees.

Metal fabricators can learn their skills on the job; certification from a trade school or community college, combined with a one- to five-year apprenticeship program, boosts employment options. The Fabricators and Manufacturers Association International (www.fmanet.org) offers continuing education courses for metalworkers.

The median salary for a metal fabricator is $37,908 per year.

Financial Services

In This Chapter

- ◆ Eco-friendly products and services that give traditional financial services jobs a green twist

- ◆ Licenses that are required to buy and sell stocks, bonds, and securities—and how to get them

- ◆ New legislation that can boost green career opportunities in the financial services industry

These days, money isn't the only thing that's green in the financial services industry. Green financial products and services have become more prevalent in recent years.

A report produced by the North American Task Force of the United Nations Environment Programme Finance Initiative (www.unepfi.org) found that options for expanding lending and financing arrangements to promote environmental issues abound—and can be found at institutions ranging from big banks and regional credit unions to asset management firms and insurance companies. Individual banking customers and multinational corporations are demanding green programs and services from their financial representatives, which has a positive impact on the economy, the environment, and the job market.

Consumer Banking

At first glance, the basic services offered in consumer banking have little to do with the environment—but that is changing. Applying for a mortgage, using a debit or credit card, buying stocks, and shopping for insurance have taken a green twist. A recent IBT Market Pulse Survey, "A Different Shade of Green" (www.ibtenterprises. com), found that 19 percent of consumer banks that responded to the survey had eco-friendly car loans, 17 percent offered green home financing, and 8 percent had green credit cards. Consumers have more options than ever to use their banking needs to have positive impacts on the environment. As a result, green careers in consumer banking are exploding.

Investment Broker

Individuals can't buy and sell stocks and securities through the stock exchange; investment brokers, also called *stockbrokers*, must handle the transactions. Their roles include executing buy and sell orders, explaining the workings of the stock exchange to clients, providing detailed information on stock performance, and gathering information from clients to determine the best investments to meet their financial goals.

After an investment broker and a client agree on which stocks and securities to buy and sell, the broker sends the order to the floor of the securities exchange, supplies the client with the price, transfers the title of the stock to the client, and finalizes the paperwork.

One of the fastest-growing areas of specialization for investment brokers is *socially responsible investing (SRI)*. In fact, $1 of every $9 under professional management is invested in socially responsible investments, totaling 11 percent of the $25.1 trillion in managed assets in the United States.

Green Guidance

For information on socially responsible investing, check out *The Complete Idiot's Guide to Socially Responsible Investing* (Alpha, 2008).

To perform their jobs, investment brokers must monitor financial markets such as *NASDAQ* and the *Dow Jones Industrial Average*, stay up-to-date on the financial dealings of the companies traded on the stock exchange, and (perhaps most importantly) develop a client base.

def•i•ni•tion

Socially responsible investing (SRI) refers to an investment strategy that maximizes financial return by investing in companies that promote corporate best practices such as environmental stewardship, human rights, and diversity. SRI can also include avoiding investing in businesses that are involved in alcohol, tobacco, gambling, and weapons. It's also called sustainable investing or ethical investing.

NASDAQ is the acronym of the National Association of Securities Dealers Automated Quotation System. It is the largest screen-based equity securities trading market in the United States and lists more than 3,200 companies. The NASDAQ has more trading volume per day than any other stock exchange in the world.

The **Dow Jones Industrial Average,** also called the Dow Jones or the Dow, is a stock market index that gauges the performance of the industrial component of U.S. stock markets. It's the second oldest continuing market in the United States, after the Dow Jones Transportation Average.

Because most investment brokers receive commission, they must find clients who need brokers to buy and sell stocks and securities on their behalf. Early in their careers, investment brokers spend a lot of time making cold calls, asking business and personal contacts for leads, and joining social and civic organizations to network with potential clients. Some investment brokers also teach financial education classes to connect with prospective clients.

The work environment for an investment broker is as varied as the companies traded on the stock exchange. In discount brokerages, which operate much the same as call centers do, investment brokers answer calls as they come in. Full-service brokerages encourage investment brokers to develop relationships with clients through face-to-face meetings and regular phone calls. In these firms, investment brokers review client needs and provide risk assessments in addition to buying and selling stocks and securities.

A college education is not required, although most investment brokers have a bachelor's degree in business administration or a related field. In the United States, investment brokers must pass the General Securities Registered Representative Examination (GSRRE)—also known as the Series 7 Exam—administered by the Financial Industry Regulatory Authority (www.finra.org).

Most states also require a second examination called the Uniform Securities Agents State Law Examination—or Series 63 or 66 exams—administered by the North

American Securities Administration Association (www.nasaa.org). Most firms offer training to help their employees pass both the Series 7 and Series 63 or 66 exams.

Investment brokers must register with FINRA, which requires a minimum of four months on the job with a registered firm and a passing grade on the GSRRE/Series 7 exam.

The job requires long hours. In fact, 25 percent of employees in the securities field work 50 or more hours per week, according to the U.S. Bureau of Labor Statistics (BLS). After-hours work to keep abreast of the markets is also common.

The median salary for an investment broker is $54,860 per year.

Mutual Fund Manager

A *mutual fund* manager implements investment strategies, invests the assets within a fund, manages day-to-day trading, and passes the proceeds from capital gains on to individual investors.

def•i•ni•tion

Mutual funds are a managed group of investments in stocks, bonds, and other securities. The fund combines money from thousands of small investors who each owns shares in the fund.

Mutual fund managers can assist with the development of new funds, set goals and directions for the funds, manage risk and portfolio allocation, establish cost structure, and address problems that might arise with funds or within the industry in which the funds are invested. Mutual fund managers also develop relationships with investors and work with the funds' boards of directors to ensure that objectives are being met.

Some mutual fund managers manage only socially responsible funds. Approximately 260 socially responsible mutual funds are available in the United States, with assets totaling $201.8 billion (up from just 55 funds with $12 billion in assets in 1995). Mutual fund managers who specialize in SRI promote and manage funds that encompass strong social and environmental principles. They help clients pick funds that reflect their individual values and financial goals.

A graduate degree is required to secure a job as a mutual fund manager. A master's degree in business administration (MBA), economics, finance, or a related field provides the best employment options.

The growth of SRIs has led a number of graduate schools to begin offering SRI courses in their MBA programs. The Haas School at the University of California at Berkley (www.haas.berkeley.edu) and the Wharton School at the University of Pennsylvania (www.wharton.upenn.edu) are just two examples of the growing number of graduate schools offering such programs to students.

Investment brokers can obtain certification as a Chartered Financial Analyst (CFA) designation through the CFA Institute (www.cfainstitute.org). To qualify, applicants must have at least four years of applicable experience and pass a series of three rigorous exams.

The BLS reports that 816,000 workers are employed in the securities, commodities, and investments industries, which include mutual fund management. Employment opportunities in financial management are expected to rise 46 percent by 2016, making it one of the fastest-growing fields in the industry.

> **Inside Scoop**
>
> The worldwide value of all mutual funds totals more than $26 trillion.

The median salary for a mutual fund manager is $148,636 per year.

Financial Planner

Financial planners advise clients on financial topics including investments, retirement planning, estate planning, tax management, and employee benefits. Their job is to help clients meet their short- and long-term financial goals, which can involve buying and selling financial products such as securities and life insurance.

Some financial planners offer comprehensive financial services, whereas others specialize in a specific aspect, such as retirement planning. A growing number of planners are focusing on SRI, helping clients make investments in companies that have strong environmental policies. Like mutual fund managers specializing in SRI, financial planners who focus on green investments promote funds that emphasize strong social and environmental principles. Financial planners research socially responsible funds and advise clients on the ones that best fit with their values and financial goals.

> **Inside Scoop**
>
> In the fiscal year ending in May 2008, inflows into green funds totaled $766 million. Alternative energy investments are among the most popular SRI category among investors.

In the course of their day, financial planners might make sales calls; meet with existing clients; develop financial plans; research investments; and consult with other professionals, including accountants, to gather information for their clients.

Job opportunities are best for a financial planner with a bachelor's degree in accounting, finance, economics, business, or related field.

Most employers require financial planners to pass the Series 7 and Series 63 or 66 exams. Obtaining a Series 7 license requires employer sponsorship, so self-employed financial advisors need to establish and maintain a connection with a large securities firm to buy and sell stocks and bonds for their clients. Financial planners who sell insurance need additional state-issued licenses.

The Certified Financial Planner (CFP) designation, issued by the Certified Financial Planner Board of Standards, Inc. (www.cfp.net), can improve job and advancement opportunities for financial advisors. CFP candidates must have a bachelor's degree, three years of relevant experience, and a passing grade on the CFP exam.

Approximately 176,000 financial planners work in the United States, with most working for banks, insurance companies, financial investment firms, and securities brokers. Thirty percent of financial planners are self-employed.

According to the BLS, opportunities for financial planners are expected to grow 41 percent by 2016, in part because of the large numbers of Americans expected to retire in the next decade. The trend of retirement savings programs (instead of traditional pension plans) also means that more people are managing their own retirement funds—and seeking the help of financial planners.

The median salary for financial planners is $66,120 per year.

Green Lender

Green lenders are mortgage brokers who specialize in helping clients secure *energy-efficient mortgages (EEMs)*. Their jobs involve gathering financial information from clients, completing application paperwork, pulling credit scores, and making mortgage loans. Green lenders must review Home Energy Rating Systems reports to ensure that homes meet energy-efficient guidelines.

def•i•ni•tion

Energy-efficient mortgages (EEMs), also called *green mortgages,* offer lower interest rates or rebates to borrowers who purchase new energy-efficient homes, invest in energy-efficient retrofits, or purchase green power. Buyers applying for EEMs can often qualify for larger loans because lenders believe energy-efficient homes will cost less to operate, freeing up monthly income that can go toward higher mortgage payments. The programs also enable buyers to finance up to 100 percent of energy-efficiency improvements.

Large lending institutions such as Bank of America, Wells Fargo, Chase Manhattan, and Citigroup all offer green mortgages; smaller lenders also offer similar programs. The market for EEMs is still fairly small, so many green lenders also offer conventional mortgages to clients.

Inside Scoop

The Green Resources for Energy-Efficient Neighborhoods (GREEN) Act, a bill that provides incentives to lenders to provide lower interest loans to those who build, buy, or remodel their homes and businesses to improve energy efficiency, is before the House of Representatives. If it passes, it could lead to more lenders offering EEMs and create more jobs for green lenders.

Green lenders need a bachelor's degree in finance, economics, or a related field. Advanced certifications such as the Loan Review Certificate Program offered by the Bank Administration Institute (www.bai.org) or the Certified Mortgage Banker designation from the Mortgage Bankers Association (www.mbaa.org) can improve career and advancement opportunities.

Most green lenders work for commercial banks, credit unions, and related financial institutions.

The median annual salary for green lenders is $51,760.

Insurance Broker

Insurance brokers work with clients to select the best policies for their needs. Their goal is to provide life, health, long-term care, property, disability, and auto policies that best meet the needs of their clients. To do this, insurance brokers might provide details about available coverage, complete application paperwork, and issue policies.

The availability of green insurance policies is growing significantly, leading insurance brokers to start specializing in eco-friendly insurance. A report by the environmental group Ceres (www.ceres.org) found that 400 new green insurance initiatives were launched in 2007—more than double the number offered just 14 months before.

Currently, green policies include pay-as-you-drive (PAYD) auto insurance premiums, carbon-neutral home/auto insurance, discounts for hybrid and fuel-efficient vehicles, and lower rates for Leadership in Energy and Environmental Design–certified buildings.

> **Inside Scoop**
>
> Pay-as-you-drive (PAYD) policies are offered by 19 insurers around the world and have been shown to reduce the overall number of miles driven by policyholders by up to 15 percent. In the United States, Progressive and GMAC offer PAYD policies.

No formal education is necessary to secure a job as an insurance broker. Insurance brokers are required to have state-issued licenses to sell health and life insurance and property and casualty insurance. In most states, an insurance broker must complete continuing education courses and pass a state examination before earning a license.

Half of all insurance brokers work for insurance agencies or brokerages, and 23 percent are employed directly by insurance carriers. Others work for banks and securities firms, and a small percentage are self-employed.

The median salary for an insurance broker is $43,870 per year.

Commercial Banking

Commercial banking focuses on providing financial services and solutions to corporations, institutions, governments, and other public entities with complex financial needs. Banks might underwrite debt, supply equity, manage funds, advise on mergers and acquisitions, and trade commodities and securities on national and international markets.

More than ever, commercial banks are turning their attention toward investing in green industries. In 2006, several prominent business leaders in California formed New Resource Bank—the nation's first commercial bank targeting green businesses—with $24.7 million in assets. Jobs in commercial banking are varied, but most have a few things in common: excellent salaries, opportunities for advancement, and the chance to use their careers to positively impact the environment.

Emissions Broker

Emissions brokers connect companies who want to buy, sell, or trade *emission reduction credits (ERCs)*. Their role is similar to that of a stockbroker; instead of stocks and securities, ERCs, also known as *offsets*, are the commodities.

def•i•ni•tion

Emission reduction credits (ERCs) are state-granted upon request to companies who reduce their emissions below required levels. Extra credits can be bought, sold, or traded to companies whose pollution levels exceed their allotted credits. Companies with extra ERCs can also bank them for future use. The credits were designed to reward companies for reducing emissions below required levels. ERCs have also helped create a framework to promote a market-based approach to emission control.

Emissions brokers identify projects that are eligible for selling and receiving ERCs, work on behalf of clients to facilitate transactions, trade credits on the Chicago Climate Exchange (www.chicagoclimatex.com), and complete required paperwork.

Currently, the job market for emissions brokers is much stronger in Europe, where countries have agreed to curb greenhouse gasses under the *Kyoto Protocol*. Opportunities in the United States are expanding at a rapid pace.

Despite the fact that the United States did not sign the Kyoto Protocol, legislation to cap emissions is inevitable. In 2008, the Warner-Lieberman bill was introduced in the Senate and aims to limit U.S. greenhouse gas emissions in 2012 to 2005 levels and reduce emissions by 70 percent in 2050.

def•i•ni•tion

The **Kyoto Protocol** is a United Nations treaty designed to reduce greenhouse gas emissions worldwide. It was adopted in 1997 and signed and ratified by 182 parties around the world.

According to the World Bank, the offset market was worth $64 billion in 2007. It's estimated that the market could be worth in excess of $3 trillion by 2020, leading to an explosion in job creation for emissions brokers.

Emissions brokers work for consulting and service firms in the United States and abroad, especially in Europe and Japan. A master's degree in business, economics, or environmental policy is required to secure a position as an emissions broker. The International Emissions Trading Association (www.ieta.org) and the Greenhouse Gas

Management Institute (www.ghginstitute.org) offer training, conferences, certifications, and networking opportunities emissions control.

Because emissions brokering is a new career, accurate salary information is difficult to obtain. According to some estimates, emissions brokers can expect to earn an average of $75,000 per year.

Investment Banker

Investment bankers advise clients on financial matters such as mergers and acquisitions, stock sales, making initial public offerings, and securing venture capital. Experienced investment bankers might manage the mergers of multibillion-dollar companies and the privatization of government assets around the world.

To do their jobs, investment bankers need to conduct extensive research and develop comprehensive financial plans for their clients.

Brokering deals for environmental companies is a growing focus in investment banking. To this end, some banks have developed entire divisions or teams dedicated to financing projects such as renewable energy and carbon credits.

Inside Scoop

JPMorgan led efforts to raise $1.5 billion in equity for the wind power market. The firm has a renewable energy portfolio that comprises $1 billion in equity investments in 26 wind farms and is pursuing investments in biomass, geothermal, and solar power. Investment bankers are at the forefront of brokering these deals.

Investment bankers can help companies develop strategies to raise capital (and ensure that funds were secured in accordance with government regulations) and prepare all the required paperwork to finalize deals. Their efforts are essential for helping clean technology providers, carbon credit developers, and other firms marketing environmental products and services reach initial public offerings (IPOs).

Several banks, including HSBC, JPMorgan, and ABN AMRO, are significantly active in pursuing deals with positive environmental impacts. In the third quarter of 2007, investment bankers helped raise more than $1.3 billion in venture capital to support clean technologies.

Investment bankers work for banks, insurance companies, private equity firms, mutual funds, and retirement or pension funds. The job can involve a significant amount of travel; 100-hour workweeks and all-night sessions before a deal closes are common, especially in the early stages of an investment banker's career.

A master's degree in business administration, finance, economics, or a related field is essential for securing a job as an investment banker. Passing the Series 7 and Series 63 or 66 exams, along with certification as a Chartered Financial Analyst (www.cfainstitute.org), can improve job prospects.

The median annual salary for an investment banker is $258,000.

Chapter 11

Business and Hospitality Services

In This Chapter

♦ New certifications and educational programs designed for green travel professionals

♦ Industries where opportunities are expanding and where job growth is flat

♦ Changes professional associations are making to highlight the greening of their industries

♦ The careers that demand long hours and weekend work

Businesses are focused on their bottom lines: in industries ranging from finance and pharmaceuticals to hotels and airlines, decision-makers are realizing that going green can keep them in the black. More than ever, service providers are being chosen for their green business practices, giving preference—and awarding lucrative contracts—to experts in the business and hospitality industries who are familiar with going green.

The environmental impact of these industries is enormous. Hotels use 38 billion kilowatts (kWh) of electricity per year and 218 gallons of water per day in every guestroom, and 17 percent of energy use in the United States is linked to food choices made by U.S. consumers—leaving a lot of room for improvement. Associations are jumping in to help make a difference. The American Hotel and Lodging Association developed a Green Task Force to help hoteliers and meeting and event planners develop shared guidelines to green all aspects of their operations. It's the professionals in these fields, though, who are having the biggest impact by using their careers to safeguard the environment.

Sustainable Tourism

Americans love to travel. Almost $700 billion is spent on travel every year in the United States, making it the largest service sector industry in the world. Now, interest in travel that has a minimal impact on the environment is stronger than ever. In fact, more than half of all Americans are more likely to select an airline, a hotel, or a rental car agency that uses environmentally friendly products and processes, according to the American Society of Travel Agents (www.asta.org). The growing demand for sustainable tourism has created job opportunities for travel agents, tour operators, and hotel managers who specialize in green travel.

Travel Agent

Travel agents work with clients to research, plan, and make travel arrangements to destinations around the globe. Travel agents do more than reserve a hotel room and coordinate transportation, though. They also act as trusted advisors to their clients, offering suggestions for the best destinations, resorts, and package tours—as well as which ones to avoid. Resorts and tour operators also work with travel agents to promote their packages.

Growing concern about the environment has led more travel agents to specialize in green travel. Green travel agents advise clients on environmental programs at hotels, make referrals to eco-friendly tour operators, and make reservations for hybrid car rentals.

> **Inside Scoop**
>
> More than 60 million Americans look for travel companies that protect and preserve the environment, and upwards of 58 million are willing to pay more to patronize these companies, according to the Travel Industry Association of America.

Travel agents also provide information on document requirements such as passports, visas, and vaccinations for various destinations; currency exchange rates; and travel advisories.

To provide accurate information to their clients, travel agents sometimes travel to the destinations they represent to gather information on accommodations, restaurants, and activities.

No formal education is required to become a travel agent, and on-the-job training is commonplace. Several community colleges offer programs for travel agents, and additional certifications are available through the National Business Travel Association (www.nbta.org). Travel agents specializing in green travel can be certified through the American Society of Travel Agents Green Member program. The program recognizes travel agents who promote green travel and lets travelers easily identify agents who can help them plan eco-friendly vacations.

Even though the demand for green travel is growing, travel agents are facing increasing competition from websites. According to the U.S. Bureau of Labor Statistics (BLS), opportunities for travel agents are expected to increase by a mere 1 percent by 2016. To improve their opportunities, travel agents are specializing in specific destinations, modes of travel (cruises or rail travel), demographic groups, or green travel.

Travel agents earn a median salary of $29,210 per year.

Tour Operator

Tour operators are responsible for designing travel packages and overseeing all aspects of trips. Their jobs can entail researching destinations, marketing packages to travelers, and leading excursions.

A tour operator might coordinate comprehensive packages that include airfare, transfers to and from a resort, accommodations, meals, and select activities for a weeklong trip. Or, a tour operator might coordinate an afternoon whitewater rafting trip that includes transportation, equipment, and guide service. In both cases, tour operators would quote an all-inclusive price for the package.

To distinguish themselves from the competition, tour operators often specialize in specific destinations, activities, modes of travel (such as cruises), or specific populations. *Ecotourism* is one of the fastest-growing segments of the travel industry, leading to a substantial increase in the number of tour operators specializing in green travel.

def•i•ni•tion

Ecotourism refers to responsible travel to natural areas that preserves the environment and improves the well-being of local people, according to the International Ecotourism Society.

Inside Scoop

Hawaii, Alaska, and Idaho have the most job opportunities for tour operators, and Wyoming, Washington, and Idaho have the highest wages in the industry.

Currently, the travel industry is the largest business sector in the world, responsible for over 230 million jobs and more than 10 percent of the gross domestic product worldwide. As a segment of the market, ecotourism is expected to increase up to 34 percent per year—three times faster than the tourism industry as a whole. Within the next five years, ecotourism could grow to 25 percent of the world's travel market, according to the International Ecotourism Society (www.ecotourism.org). Opportunities are expected to increase more quickly than the average for all occupations, according to BLS.

Tour operators often work irregular hours, including evenings and weekends. The job requires a significant amount of time away from the office, researching new tours, leading trips, and attending trade shows to meet with prospective clients.

No formal education is required to become a tour operator. The National Tour Association (www.ntaonline.com) offers designation as a Certified Tour Professional that can boost career opportunities. The United States Tour Operators Association (www.ustoa.com) organizes conferences and networking events for members on all aspects of the profession, including ecotourism. George Washington University has partnered with the International Ecotourism Society to offer courses in ecotourism.

The median salary for a tour operator is $26,500 per year.

Hotel Manager

Hotel managers oversee all aspects of hotel operations from hiring staff to ensuring guest satisfaction. Their duties often include office administration, marketing and sales, purchasing, maintenance, and staff scheduling and training. The overall goal of their jobs is to ensure efficient and profitable hotel operations.

Hotel managers are at the forefront of making lodgings more eco-friendly. Implementing linen reuse programs, installing energy-efficient features such as compact fluorescent lights (CFLs) and low-flow showerheads, and switching to non-toxic cleaning products are just a few of the things hotel managers can do to lessen the environmental impact of the properties they manage. Some hotel managers go a step further, pushing for solar power, offering climate-neutral rooms, and offsetting their carbon emissions. For their efforts, hotel managers can seek certification from Sustainable Travel International (www.sustainabletravelinternational.org) and GreenSeal (www.greenseal.org), organizations that offer independent ratings of green products and services.

Hotel managers, as the title suggests, often work in hotels and motels. The properties might be small, independently owned lodgings or part of an international chain of hotels. Bed-and-breakfasts, hostels, and RV parks also employ hotel managers.

Approximately 71,000 hotel managers work in the United States, and more than half—54 percent—are self-employed as the owners of small hotels and bed-and-breakfasts. Employment is expected to grow 12 percent by 2016.

> ### Inside Scoop
>
> The website www.environmentallyfriendlyhotels.com rates green hotels around the world based on 29 eco-friendly criteria, such as composting programs and linen reuse programs. More than 2,800 hotels are currently listed on the site.

Small hotels are often willing to hire hotel managers with no formal education and to provide on-the-job training. High-end properties, resorts, and full-service hotel chains look for hotel managers with bachelor's degrees in business or hotel and hospitality management.

The increased emphasis on green hotel operations has led a number of schools to begin offering courses focusing on sustainable property management and hospitality. The Cornell School of Hotel Administration has a course called Sustainable Development and the Global Hospitality Industry; Florida International University has undergraduate courses in sustainable tourism; and graduate students in the Department of Tourism at George Washington University can major in sustainable management.

High school students interested in careers in hotel management can get a jump-start on their education through the Lodging Management Program created by the Educational Institute of the American Hotel & Lodging Association (www.ahla.com). The two-year program is offered at 450 high schools in 45 states and allows students to earn professional certifications as Certified Rooms Division Specialists as well as credits that can be used toward a college degree in hotel management.

The median annual salary for a hotel manager is $42,320.

Meetings and Events

Conferences, trade shows, annual meetings, and corporate retreats are part of the corporate culture in the United States. Coordinating multifaceted events like these requires the assistance of experts, and making these events more eco-friendly has created job opportunities for experts who understand how to produce top-notch events with minimal environmental impacts. Growth in the fields of meeting and event planning and catering and food service management are strong, allowing newcomers and career-changers chances to enter the field and giving experienced professionals new opportunities to expand their skills and explore a novel aspect of these industries.

Meeting and Event Planner

Meeting and event planners are responsible for coordinating all aspects of meetings, conventions, and special events. Their duties include securing a location, negotiating contracts, configuring the space, hiring contractors (such as caterers and florists), and providing overall event management to ensure things run smoothly. To accomplish these goals, meeting and event planners work closely with their clients.

In organizations with offices around the United States—or around the globe—meeting and event planners may be asked to coordinate virtual events using tools such as videoconferencing, which is a much more eco-friendly option than flying across the country for a meeting.

Greening meetings and events has become a growing trend, and career opportunities for planners are increasing as a result. Businesses are turning to meeting and event planners to coordinate events that have minimal impact on the environment. To this end, planners are using electronic promotion and registration materials; hosting events in buildings certified by Leadership in Energy and Environmental Design (LEED); ensuring that venues have established recycling programs; printing materials on recycled paper with vegetable-based ink; and asking speakers to e-mail handouts to participants that request them, instead of printing out copies for all attendees.

> **Inside Scoop**
>
> A survey conducted by *Special Events Magazine* (www.specialevents.com) found that 75 percent of planners add some green elements to their events; 16 percent coordinate events that are as eco-friendly as possible.

The U.S. Environmental Protection Agency (EPA) has created a program to help meeting and event planners coordinate green events. The One-Stop Information Source for Green Meetings (www.epa.gov/oppt/greenmeetings) includes tips for planning green meetings and events.

The Green Meeting Industry Council (www.greenmeetings.info) is another resource available to meeting and event planners who want to minimize the environmental impacts of the events they coordinate. The council hosts annual conferences and is in the process of developing a certification program for green meeting and event planners.

Landing a job as a meeting and event planner requires a bachelor's degree in public relations, communications, marketing, business, hospitality management, or a related field. Several universities offer bachelor's and master's degrees in meetings management.

Designation as a Certified Meeting Professional is offered through the Convention Industry Council (www.conventionindustry.org) and can improve job options for meeting and event planners. To qualify, candidates need at least three years of meeting or event management experience, full-time employment in the profession, and passing grades on the required exams.

Meeting and event planners who want to work for the government can benefit from earning a credential as a Certified Government Meeting Professional through the Society of Government Meeting Professionals (www.sgmp.org). Professional associations such as the International Special Events Society (www.ises.com) and Meeting Professionals International (www.mpiweb.org) offer professional development and networking opportunities to members.

More than 51,000 meeting and event planners work in the United States. Approximately 27 percent are employed by civic, religious, and professional organizations; 17 percent work for hotels and convention centers; 3 percent work for governments; and 6 percent are self-employed.

Opportunities in the meeting and event planning field are expected to grow 20 percent by 2016. The BLS predicts that the majority of new jobs will be in the medical and pharmaceutical industries, including private companies and professional associations.

The median salary for a meeting and event planner is $42,180 per year.

Caterer/Food Service Manager

Caterers and food service managers oversee all food-related aspects at events and organizations. Working in schools, hospitals, hotels, factories, and private companies, caterers and food service managers create menus, purchase food and supplies, deal with vendors, and supervise staff.

As organizations become more focused on their environmental impacts, the demand for green catering and food service management has been skyrocketing. Caterers and food service managers are turning to local and organic foods, using biodegradable dinnerware, storing foods in reusable containers, and composting food scraps. Currently, more than 75 percent of food service agencies purchase products made from recycled materials, according to the National Restaurant Association. Other environmentally friendly initiatives in the food service industry include recycling cooking oils, glassware, aluminum cans, and paper products.

> ### Inside Scoop
>
> Americans send more than 85 million tons of paper products, including paper plates, to landfills every year. Caterers and food service managers who replace paper plates with dinnerware made from potato starch, sugarcane, and corn plastic can significantly cut waste.

There are 9.4 million food service workers in the United States, including an estimated 149,000 food service managers and 115,000 caterers. In this field, employees commonly work long hours, including evenings and weekends. Often, caterers are on call and need to report to work with little notice.

The educational requirements for caterers and food service managers are varied. Sometimes, a high school diploma is enough to enter the field. Graduating from culinary school or earning a bachelor's degree in culinary arts or hospitality is necessary for some positions, and a master's degree in hospitality is often required to secure a management position. The American Culinary Federation (www.acfchefs.org) accredits more than 200 training and apprenticeship programs around the country.

The median salary for caterers and food service managers is $34,370 per year.

Wedding Coordinator

Wedding coordinators work with engaged couples to plan all aspects of their weddings. Their duties can include securing ceremony and reception sites; interviewing caterers; providing referrals for music, flowers, and other services; coordinating audio-visual requirements; setting timelines; and troubleshooting on the day of the event.

Wedding coordinators, also called wedding planners or wedding consultants, are part of a growing trend toward eco-friendly weddings. Couples who want to plan green weddings often turn to wedding coordinators for their vast network of resources. Wedding coordinators can minimize the environmental impacts of their clients' weddings by securing venues with comprehensive environmental policies that include purchasing renewable energy, using nontoxic cleaning products, and maintaining recycling programs; and making referrals to printers that use recycled paper and non-toxic ink for invitations, florists who supply organic blooms, and caterers whose menus include organic and locally grown foods.

Wedding coordinators can work for hotels, convention centers, country clubs, or bridal consulting businesses. Many wedding coordinators are also self-employed. They divide their time between working in an office and traveling to meet with clients and service providers.

The job entails working long hours, including evenings and weekends, especially during "wedding season" between the months of May and October. It's also common for wedding coordinators to plan several weddings at the same time. During off-peak months, wedding coordinators often participate in bridal shows to promote their services and meet with potential clients, tour new venues, and meet with service providers such as caterers and florists to learn about new offerings.

There are no formal educational requirements to become a wedding coordinator. Those who are self-employed may benefit from earning a bachelor's degree in business administration or marketing. Several community colleges offer certificates in wedding planning. The Association of Certified Professional Wedding Consultants (www.acpwc.com) also offers certification programs.

The average annual salary for a wedding coordinator is $31,000.

Small Business Opportunities

In This Chapter

- Franchises that are going green, leading to job opportunities with nationally recognized companies

- The growing field of green energy that has created new careers for sales professionals

- The demand for organic and local foods, which allows chefs to combine their passion for food with their love of the environment

- Legislation that is paving the way for an increase in the number of eco-friendly dry cleaners

- A new certification that is helping real estate agents go green

Small businesses are the backbone of America. According to the U.S. Small Business Administration (www.sba.gov), 52 percent of businesses in the United States are small businesses that account for more than half of the private, nonfarm gross domestic product in the United States. Directing even a fraction of those profits toward launching and supporting green businesses would give a significant boost to the green economy and help build a more sustainable future.

Currently, up to 80 percent of the new jobs created every year in the United States is in small businesses. Small businesses can be found in every sector of the economy and offer careers ranging from entry-level manual labor jobs to executive positions that require advanced degrees and years of experience.

More small businesses than ever are embracing green business practices, offering green services, and selling green products, which means it's easier than ever to find a green career in a small business.

Design and Innovation

Designing green products is big business. On average, Americans spend $2.5 billion on transportation, food, clothing, and home accessories per year. As the demand for green products increases, so do careers for designers who know how to use eco-friendly materials to create innovative new products.

Careers in this field range from traditional 9-to-5 jobs with creative corporations to irregular hours doing freelance design work. A good place to start looking for a career in green design is www.sustainablebusiness.com, where you can see which companies made the SB20, a list of the top 20 innovative companies focused on sustainable design and business.

Industrial Designer

Industrial designers invent new products. Their goal is to use their knowledge of art, business, and engineering to design products that are stylish and functional.

Industrial designers conduct market research; meet with clients to determine the desired product characteristics, such as size, shape, weight, color, and materials; prepare conceptual sketches; create prototypes; and present designs to clients and adjust the designs based on their feedback. Often, industrial designers work alongside engineers and accountants to find methods for making products easier to assemble, safer to use, and cheaper to manufacture.

The growing demand for green products has led industrial designers to explore options for using environmentally friendly materials. Specifically, industrial designers might research options for manufacturing water bottles from stainless steel instead of plastic or for making T-shirts from organic cotton instead of conventional cotton.

Industrial designers often specialize in a particular product or category, such as appliances, technology, furniture, toys, or housewares.

Industrial designers work for manufacturing companies, corporations, and design firms. Freelance and contract work are also popular options, with 30 percent of the 48,000 industrial designers in the United States working on a freelance basis.

Most industrial designers work 40 hours per week, although working outside of a regular 9-to-5 schedule is common. To meet deadlines and attend client meetings, industrial designers often work in the evenings and on weekends. Freelance designers tend to work longer hours to earn a living. Travel to manufacturing companies, design centers, client sites, and testing facilities is often required.

Career Crisis

A growing number of products is being designed and manufactured outside the United States, resulting in fewer opportunities for industrial designers. The U.S. Bureau of Labor Statistics (BLS) predicts job growth will increase a mere 7 percent by 2016. The number of opportunities for industrial designers might decrease further if design work continues to be outsourced to companies located overseas.

A bachelor's degree in industrial design, architecture, or engineering is the minimum requirement to work as an industrial designer.

The Industrial Designers Society of America (www.idsa.org), the Professional Industrial Design Association (www.freelancedesigners.com), and the Association of Women Industrial Designers (www.awidweb.com) all host conferences and design competitions and provide job listings for members.

The annual median wage for industrial designers is $56,550.

Furniture Maker

Furniture makers build furniture. The job entails reading design blueprints; selecting materials; cutting, shaping, and preparing wood pieces; and assembling the finished products. Furniture makers often build one-of-a-kind pieces using precision tools and detailed finishing techniques.

To minimize the environmental impact of their products, more furniture makers are opting for green wood products, such as recycled or salvaged woods, bamboo, or wood that comes from well-managed forests. The Sustainable Woods Network (www.sustainablewoods.net) is a clearinghouse for wood that comes from sustainably harvested woodlands.

To do their jobs, furniture makers use hand and machine tools, like computerized numerical control (CNC) machines, that enable them to create complex furniture designs while increasing production speed.

The working conditions for furniture makers include heavy lifting; excessive noise, dust, and air pollutants; and the risk of injury from power tools, sharp tools, and rough lumber. To minimize the risks, furniture makers often wear earplugs, safety glasses, and dust masks.

There are 370,000 furniture makers in the United States. Most work for furniture manufacturers, specialty furniture retailers, and repair shops, although a small percentage of furniture makers are self-employed. Opportunities for furniture makers are expected to decline over the next decade, due in part to increased automation, mass production, and a strong import market.

There are no formal educational requirements to become a furniture maker, with on-the-job training being the norm. Furniture makers can enroll in degree programs offered at vocational and trade schools that teach the basics of production management, wood engineering, and furniture manufacturing.

Regional associations such as the New Hampshire Furniture Masters Association (www.furnituremasters.org) and the Norfolk Furniture Makers Association (www.norfolkfurnituremakers.org) offer networking opportunities to members.

The median salary for a furniture maker is $25,820 per year.

Clothing Designer

Clothing designers create concepts for clothing, footwear, and accessories. Their job is to research fashion trends, sketch designs of clothing and accessories, choose colors and fabrics, make prototypes and patterns, oversee clothing production, and market their designs to retailers. The initial designs are often sketched by hand and then translated to the computer using computer-aided design.

Some clothing designers have turned their attention to designing clothes made from environmentally friendly fabrics such as organic cotton, bamboo, soy, hemp, jute, and modal. Companies such as Nike (www.nike.com), American Apparel (www. americanapparel.net), and Patagonia (www.patagonia.com) have all begun manufacturing clothes out of eco-friendly fabrics, creating more opportunities for clothing designers who want to work for established brands.

Clothing designers, also called *fashion designers*, often specialize in a specific aspect of design, like jeans, sportswear, accessories, or footwear. Some clothing designers market their designs through their own retail stores; others join design co-ops, sell to small boutiques, or establish relationships with major retailers. A small percentage of clothing designers create custom designs for clients, called *haute couture*, or high fashion.

Inside Scoop
It takes approximately one-third of a pound of chemicals to grow enough cotton for one conventional cotton T-shirt, according to the Sustainable Cotton Project (www.sustainablecotton.org).

Clothing designers work for design firms, wholesalers, and clothing manufacturers, although freelance and contract work is common. Most clothing designers work a regular 9-to-5 schedule, but night and weekend work might be required to meet production deadlines, prepare for fashion shows, or meet with suppliers. The job can also involve extensive travel both across the United States and around the world to attend trade and fashion shows, meet with clients, and find sources for new materials.

There are 20,000 clothing designers in the United States. Almost one-third work for apparel wholesalers; clothing stores, design firms, and performing arts companies also employ a large number of clothing designers. Many clothing designers, however, are self-employed. Opportunities tend to be centered in urban areas such as New York and Los Angeles.

A bachelor's degree in fine arts, fashion design, or a related field is often required to work as a clothing designer, especially in an established design firm. A growing number of clothing designers, especially those who want to own their own boutiques, are pursuing master's degrees in marketing or fashion merchandising to improve their business knowledge.

The American Apparel and Footwear Association (www.apparelandfootwear.org) and International Apparel Federation (www.iafnet.org) offer events, resources, and information about legislative actions related to apparel design and manufacturing.

Clothing designers earn a median annual salary of $62,810.

Sales and Distribution

Sales and distribution is an essential part of introducing green products and services to the masses. Consumers are fueling the demand for green products, asking retailers and service providers to consider the environment when making decisions about the products they stock and the services they offer—and it's working. The market for green products and services is bigger than ever.

Whether products travel across the country or across town to the shelves of major retailers or local boutiques, one thing remains the same: their availability is crucial to the expansion of the green economy.

Franchisee

Franchisees own and operate local branches of national *franchises*, including fast-food restaurants, dry cleaners, shipping companies, and staffing services. The responsibilities of a franchisee are varied depending on the type of franchise he owns. In general, a franchisee oversees all aspects of running a business, from ordering supplies and hiring staff to marketing products and services to ensuring customer satisfaction. A franchisee might also handle bookkeeping duties, distribution, and facilities maintenance.

def•i•ni•tion

Franchises are national companies with established customer bases and methods of conducting business. Franchisees enter into contracts to use the franchise name on a nonexclusive basis to sell goods or services.

Several green franchises, including Energy Doctor (www.energydoctorinc.com), a national distributor of products to help homeowners reduce their energy costs; Solar Power, Inc. (www.solarpowerinc.net), solar panel manufacturers and installers; and AAMCO Transmissions (www.aamco.com), an auto service business, have started recycling solvents, using water-based cleaners, and promoting alternative fuels. Even Subway (www.subway.com) is going green, trading its Styrofoam cups for eco-friendly polypropylene, stocking 100 percent recycled napkins, and installing energy-efficient heating and cooling systems in several of its stores.

An estimated 750,000 franchise businesses in the United States employ more than 18 million people. They are available in industries ranging from fast food and auto care to lawn services and pet products.

Unlike other startups, franchises have the advantage of instant brand recognition, national marketing campaigns, and training and support from the franchisor. The startup costs for a franchise are varied; according to some estimates, the initial costs to start a franchise are $250,000 plus real estate.

The startup costs include licensing fees for the use of trademarks, advertising support, and training from the franchisor, as well as supplies. In return for national support, franchisees agree to pay a fee and/or a percentage of their sales. Typically, franchise agreements last between 5 and 20 years with penalties for early cancellation.

There are no formal educational requirements to become a franchisee; a bachelor's degree in business, finance, or a related field can be beneficial. Most franchisors also require new franchisees to attend training classes to learn all aspects of the business prior to opening the franchise.

The International Franchise Association (www.franchise.org) and the American Franchisee Association (www.franchisee.org) offer classes, support, and networking opportunities to members. In addition, several regional franchise associations enable local franchisees to connect with each other and discuss challenges and successes.

There are no reliable statistics on the annual wages of franchisees.

Distribution Manager

Distribution managers handle all aspects of product distribution including storage, transportation, and delivery. Their job is to ensure that green products, such as organic produce, organic cotton T-shirts, compact florescent light (CFL) bulbs, and terra-cotta pots, are transported from the manufacturers to the retailers.

The responsibilities of a distribution manager include scheduling deliveries; overseeing shipping and receiving; maintaining inventory levels; administering the distribution budget; managing the warehouse; hiring, training, and supervising distribution staff; and ensuring that safety standards are being met. The job might require coordinating activities with other departments such as warehouse and transportation managers.

Distribution managers work for warehouses, manufacturing companies, and retail outlets. Most work 40 hours per week, although shift work is common because warehouses often run on 24-hour schedules. The job involves lifting, bending, and standing for long periods of time.

There are 94,000 distribution managers in the United States, and job growth is expected to remain stagnant in the coming decade—in large part due to increased automation.

Most positions require a high school diploma and warehouse experience, although some companies look for candidates with a bachelor's degree in business, logistics, or a related field.

The Distribution Business Management Association (www.dcenter.com) hosts an annual conference for distribution professionals.

The median annual wage for distribution managers is $33,870.

Energy Sales Representative

Energy sales representatives promote renewable energy products such as solar, wind, and geothermal energy and sign up new commercial and residential clients for services. Their responsibilities include establishing sales goals, meeting with prospective clients, responding to customer inquiries, explaining the benefits of renewable energy, enrolling new accounts, processing paperwork, and ensuring ongoing customer satisfaction.

Energy sales representatives might contact existing customers about renewing their contracts at the ends of the sales terms and try to win back customers who have canceled their business. In some cases, they also work with marketing teams to develop new promotions and attend trade shows.

A growing number of private companies and utilities are offering renewable energy options to commercial and residential customers, creating a wealth of new job opportunities for energy sales representatives.

Energy sales representatives require a minimum of a bachelor's degree in marketing, finance, economics, or a related field.

Energy associations such as the American Wind Energy Association (www.awea.org), the Geothermal Energy Association (www.geo-energy.org), and the United States Energy Association (www.usea.org) can help energy sales representatives stay abreast of all the latest news in the field.

Energy sales representatives often work on commission, although they earn median annual salaries of $70,040.

Food and Beverages

Global sales of organic food and beverages topped $40 billion in 2006, making it one of the fastest-growing segments of the green economy. Legislation is supporting the growth of the organic food and beverage market, providing funds to support its production, processing, and distribution. Illinois has passed the Illinois Local and Organic Food and Farm Task Force to promote sustainable local food production across the state; Vermont, New York, and North Carolina are among a handful of other states pursuing legislation to increase the production and distribution of local and organic foods. The payoffs are evident: sales of organic food and beverages are increasing 15 percent per year and currently account for 3 percent of food sales in the United States. Thus, it's a good time to pursue a career in the green food and beverage industry.

Brewmaster

Brewmasters oversee the entire beer brewing process. Their role includes formulating recipes, ordering ingredients like hops and grain, brewing beer, tasting beer samples, and directing taproom operations. Brewmasters also manage inventory levels and hire, train, and supervise brewery staff. They might also lead beer tastings, offer tours of the brewery, and participate in special events.

A growing number of brewmasters are brewing organic beers. Organic beers are made from organically grown hops, malt, barley, and natural yeast. Brewmasters at *microbreweries* are the biggest producers of organic beers, but large breweries such as Anheuser-Busch are also developing organic brews.

def•i•ni•tion

Microbreweries are breweries that produce fewer than 15,000 barrels of beer per year. Currently, there are 1,500 microbreweries in the United States; California, Colorado, and Texas have more microbreweries than any other states in the country.

The Beer Institute (www.beerinstitute.org) anticipates 1.5 percent growth over the next decade, leading to more opportunities for brewmasters.

There are no formal educational requirements for brewmasters.

The Institute of Brewing & Distilling (www.ibd.org.uk) is based in London but offers a diploma in Brewing Modules that has international recognition. The school graduates approximately 60 brewers per year.

The American Brewers Guild (www.abgbrew.com) offers online courses in craft brewing and brewing science.

The Brewers Association (www.beertown.org) hosts conferences and events and hands out awards.

Brewmasters earn an average annual wage of $34,000.

Chef

Chefs prepare dishes such as appetizers, entrées, and desserts for diners. On the job, their duties include creating new recipes, developing menus, ordering ingredients, cooking meals, and overseeing food preparation and presentation. They also hire, train, and supervise kitchen staff.

A growing number of chefs are using organic and locally grown ingredients, including fruits and vegetables, meat and seafood, and wines. Some chefs are taking their commitments to organic foods one step further, opening restaurants serving dishes that are 100 percent local and organic.

Several types of chefs exist. Executive chefs manage all kitchen operations, from ordering ingredients to overseeing food presentation; sous chefs work under executive chefs and run the kitchen in their absences; and pastry chefs are responsible for creating desserts.

Chefs work for restaurants, hotels, hospitals, cafeterias, and cruise lines. The job can require long hours, including early mornings and late nights as well as weekends and holidays.

There are 115,000 chefs in the United States. Opportunities are expected to increase 11 percent by 2016 with the best careers available in casual restaurants, as opposed to fine-dining establishments, according to the U.S. Bureau of Labor Statistics (BLS).

Although there are no formal educational requirements to become a chef, the best opportunities are available to chefs who have graduated from culinary school. The American Culinary Federation (www.acfchefs.org) accredits more than 200 culinary programs across the country.

Several professional associations are dedicated to promoting the work of trained chefs, including the Professional Chefs Association (www.professionalchef.com), the Research Chefs Association (www.culinology.com), and the American Personal & Private Chef Association (www.personalchef.com).

Chefs earn a median wage of $37,160 per year.

Services

The number of green service providers has increased dramatically. Small businesses like dry cleaners, real estate companies, printers, and even funeral services are going green, making it possible to find green businesses—and careers—in almost every sector of the service industry.

Careers in this industry are so varied that you can launch a green career, green an existing career, or make a career change into a green field—all without looking outside the service sector.

Dry Cleaner

Dry cleaners launder clothing, including leather, suede, and fur, as well as other articles, such as rugs, blankets, and draperies that require special care. They might also treat stains and make minor repairs. Dry cleaners are responsible for recording special cleaning instructions; dry cleaning, pressing, or steaming clothing; packaging items for customers; and preparing itemized bills.

There are 239,000 dry cleaners in the United States, most of which use traditional cleaning methods that involve harsh solvents such as perchloroethylene (perc), a harmful pollutant that poses a hazard to the environment, according to the U.S. Environmental Protection Agency (EPA). A growing number of dry cleaners are implementing green cleaning methods such as *wet cleaning* and *CO_2 cleaning*.

def•i•ni•tion _____

Wet cleaning uses water and specialized detergents in computer-controlled washers and dryers instead of harsh chemicals. The process generates no hazardous waste or air pollution and reduces the potential for water and soil contamination. The EPA (www. epa.gov) considers it one of the safest professional cleaning methods.

CO_2 cleaning cleans clothes using nontoxic liquid CO_2. During the cleaning process, just 2 percent of the CO_2 is released into the atmosphere, minimizing the impact on global warming compared with traditional dry cleaning.

According to the BLS, opportunities in dry cleaning will increase 10 percent by 2016, especially for dry cleaners using nontoxic cleaning methods. Legislation requiring dry cleaners to phase out the use of perc will help improve opportunities for green dry cleaners. Currently, California has passed legislation to eliminate the use of perc by 2023; New York and Massachusetts are considering similar legislation.

There are no formal educational requirements for dry cleaners.

The Drycleaning & Laundry Institute (www.ifi.org) offers continuing education classes, including instruction on wet cleaning, to members. In addition, several regional dry cleaning associations provide legislative news and events for members.

Dry cleaners earn an average of $8.58 per hour.

Printer

Printers are responsible for the preparation and processing of printed materials such as brochures, business cards, maps, letterhead, and books. Their responsibilities might include discussing project specifications with clients; preparing materials for printing; running the actual printing process; and managing the post-press process, which includes folding, binding, and trimming materials to ensure readiness for distribution.

Some printers specialize in certain products such as business cards or signs, whereas others focus on a specific type of printing, like offset or letterpress. Some printers offer quick-print services for documents, embossing, and binding. A growing number of printers are choosing to specialize in green printing, a process that minimizes the environmental impact of the printing process.

At a minimum, green printers use vegetable- or soy-based inks, print on recycled paper, and use digital technologies that create less waste than traditional printing methods. Several green printers have also opted to begin waterless printing, a process that eliminates the use of chemicals and water in the printing process.

Printers often work in large manufacturing plants with complex machines, but a growing number of boutique printing agencies specialize in specific products such as wedding invitations. Overtime can be required to meet production deadlines, and printers might need to work shifts at printing companies that run 24-hour schedules.

There are 636,000 printers in the United States, making it one of the largest manufacturing industries, although perhaps not for long. The BLS estimates a 22 percent decrease in job opportunities over the next decade due, in

> **Inside Scoop**
>
> Producing one ton of virgin uncoated paper—which accounts for 90 percent of the paper used in the United States—requires three tons of wood and 19,075 gallons of water and generates 2,278 pounds of solid waste, according to the Environmental Defense Fund (www.environmentaldefense.org).

part, to increased automation. Demand is expected to remain strong for printers who perform specialized manual tasks, such as paste-up workers, film strippers, and plate-makers.

Warning

Printing companies are reporting fewer equipment-related injuries as a result of using fewer chemicals and toxic solutions, according to the BLS. Printers still face the risk of injuries while working with printing machines, though. Last year, there were 4.2 cases of injuries per 100 workers. Although that figure is lower than the average of 6.0 cases in other manufacturing industries, it's still important for printers to take extra precautions on the job.

There are no formal education requirements to work as a printer; most training happens on the job. Several colleges offer associate degrees in printing technology that could boost employment opportunities.

The Specialty Graphic Imaging Association (www.sgia.org) offers several web-based education classes on digital printing, screen making, and corporate sustainability. The association also hosts trade shows and provides industry resources to its members.

The median hourly wage for a printer is $15.76.

Real Estate Agent

Real estate agents help clients buy and sell residential, commercial, and industrial properties. Their jobs entail researching the real estate market, developing relationships with buyers and sellers, showing properties, presenting offers and counteroffers, negotiating on behalf of their clients, and closing real estate deals.

Real estate agents might also arrange for title searches to verify property ownership; make referrals to lenders, home inspectors, and movers; and ensure environmental issues like lead paint and asbestos are resolved. Some real estate agents also rent and manage properties.

Real estate agents who want to green their careers can opt to earn the EcoBroker designation offered by EcoBroker International (www.ecobroker.com). To earn the designation, agents must take a series of online courses on environmental housing issues, such as sustainable design and indoor air quality. EcoBrokers are able to advise clients on all aspects of greening their homes, from installing solar panels to shopping for nontoxic paint. They are also able to explain the green features of a home to prospective buyers. There are 1,700 EcoBrokers in the United States, Canada, and the Caribbean.

Real estate agents work for large firms or boutique agencies and might also work for new home builders. The job involves a significant amount of driving to show clients available properties. For this reason, many real estate agents have mobile offices and might answer calls, send e-mails, and book appointments while they're on the road. Most real estate agents also have home offices.

There is no such thing as a 40-hour workweek for real estate agents. The job requires long hours including evenings, weekends, and holidays; most real estate agents are on call to meet the needs of their clients.

There are 564,000 real estate agents in the United States, and opportunities are expected to increase 11 percent, creating 62,040 new jobs by 2016. The profession is vulnerable to significant ups and downs based on economic factors such as interest rates and unemployment rates. During the next seven years, real estate agents will earn less commission, although the BLS reports that some agents leave the profession altogether during economic downturns.

Real estate agents need a high school diploma, although a bachelor's degree in business, economics, or finance increases job prospects. All 50 states and the District of Columbia also require real estate agents to have a real estate license. To earn a license, agents must complete between 30 and 90 hours of classroom instruction in real estate fundamentals such as mortgage financing, the legal aspects of buying and selling, and property inspections and must pass a written exam.

The National Association of Realtors (www.realtor.org) provides business tools, supports pro-real estate legislation, hosts an annual conference, and maintains a database of up-to-the-minute news on the national real estate market.

Real estate agents earn commission, so their salaries fluctuate from month to month based on the overall number of homes they've sold. According to the BLS, real estate agents earn a median annual salary of $58,860.

Funeral Director

Funeral directors handle all aspects of funeral preparation. The job entails transporting the deceased to the funeral home; preparing the remains; and coordinating the memorial service, funeral, and burial.

Funeral directors, also called *morticians* or *undertakers*, also work with families to ensure that the final wishes of the deceased are honored. They might be asked to prepare obituaries to be published in newspapers, arrange for pallbearers, decorate the site for the funeral services, and provide transportation for mourners. Funeral directors also oversee the shipment of the deceased for out-of-state burials.

Concern for the environment has extended to funeral services, leading to more requests for green burials. Funeral directors might suggest cardboard, bamboo, or jute coffins or biodegradable urns and might encourage cremation over burial.

Inside Scoop

Traditional burials have a significant impact on the environment. Bodies are embalmed with formaldehyde-based fluids, caskets are not biodegradable, and cemeteries are maintained with pesticides and toxic fertilizers. According to the Green Burial Council (www.greenburialcouncil.org), on an annual basis, caskets in the United States contain enough metal to build a new Golden Gate Bridge and enough concrete to pave a two-lane road from Indianapolis to New York.

Funeral directors oversee all the paperwork that is required for a formal death certificate to be issued. Sometimes, funeral directors work with those who want to plan their funerals in advance. In small funeral homes, funeral directors might also handle business matters such as preparing and sending invoices for services and marketing their services.

Funerals are often performed in funeral homes, although funeral directors might offer services in private homes or at gravesites, places of worship, or cemeteries.

There are 29,000 funeral directors in the United States, and opportunities are expected to increase 12 percent in the next decade. The job involves long hours, including evenings and weekends, and might even entail being on call. In some cases, funeral directors work shifts.

Funeral directors need to complete a degree in mortuary science. Several community colleges offer two- and four-year programs that are accredited by the American Board of Funeral Service Education (www.abfse.org).

All 50 states and the District of Columbia require funeral directors to be licensed. The requirements for licensing are varied, although most call for applicants to be at least 21 years old, have a minimum of two years of formal education, complete a one-year apprenticeship, and pass a written exam.

The Green Burial Council provides resources for funeral directors who want to promote green burials and educate their clients about the benefits. The National Funeral Directors Association (www.nfda.org) offers resources for funeral directors.

Funeral directors earn a median salary of $49,620 per year.

Lawn Care Technician

Lawn care technicians handle all aspects of residential lawn care, including fertilizing, weed and pest control, aeration, and pH balancing. Their responsibilities include applying fertilizer, treating weeds and pests, scheduling follow-up visits, and ensuring customer satisfaction.

Lawn care technicians might also be required to make sales calls, meet with homeowners to assess their lawn care needs, and suggest annual maintenance plans.

More lawn care services and landscaping companies are transitioning to green products, such as nontoxic pest and weed control and organic fertilizers, increasing the number of job opportunities for lawn care technicians who want to green their careers.

Lawn care technicians work for landscaping and lawn care companies. The job entails traveling to homes within a given region, and working irregular hours, including evenings and weekends, might be required. The work also involves working outdoors, often in extreme temperatures. In some cases, the job is seasonal; lawn care technicians might work from March to October during the peak lawn and garden season.

There are 202,000 lawn care technicians in the United States, and the growing number of homeowners is expected to increase opportunities in the field by 18 percent in the next decade, according to the BLS.

There are no formal educational requirements to become a lawn care technician, although most companies look for candidates with a high school diploma or GED and a valid driver's license.

The Professional Landcare Network (www.landcarenetwork.org) offers several certifications for lawn care technicians, including Certified Turf Grass Professional, as well as other information on the greening of the industry.

The median wage for a lawn care technician is $9.82 per hour.

Graphic Designer

Graphic designers use visual tools to communicate ideas. Their projects might include designing billboards, magazines, packaging, logos, brochures, and interactive tools such as websites, all with the goal of using images to convey an idea.

The daily duties of a graphic designer include assessing client needs; gathering information about budgets and timelines; preparing sketches to illustrate the concept; selecting colors, fonts, artwork, and other visual elements for the design; and creating page layouts. Graphic designers might also meet with creative directors and marketing managers to brainstorm creative concepts, work with printers to select paper and ink for the project, and review mock-ups for errors. Freelance graphic designers and those who run their own firms might spend a significant amount of time prospecting for new clients.

In an effort to green their careers, graphic designers are designing materials to be printed on recycled paper with soy- or vegetable-based inks. Some graphic designers are taking their commitment to the environment one step further, specializing in working with environmental groups, renewable energy companies, and green retailers to create newsletters, billboards, brochures, websites, and other marketing materials to promote their products and services.

There are 261,000 graphic designers in the United States. Some work for design firms, advertising agencies, or publishers; about 25 percent of graphic designers work on a freelance or contract basis. Most graphic designers work 40 hours per week, although overtime might be required to meet deadlines. Freelance graphic designers also tend to work longer hours to make a living.

A bachelor's degree in fine arts or graphic design is required to work as a graphic designer; some graphic designers opt to pursue a master's degree in fine art or design to improve their job prospects with large agencies.

The American Institute of Graphic Arts (www.aiga.org), the Graphic Artists Guild (www.gag.org), and the Graphic Professionals Resource Network (www.iaphc.org) provide resources to graphic designers, including news of grants and design competitions.

The median annual salary for a graphic designer is $41,280.

Writer

Writers produce original written materials such as books, magazine articles, press releases, newsletters, and brochures. Their work extends beyond just print collateral, though. Writers also produce scripts for documentaries and television commercials and write for blogs and websites. Their responsibilities include researching ideas, following up on leads, conducting interviews, organizing and writing articles, and working with editors to revise the material—all under deadline.

Several areas of specialization are available for writers, including fiction, nonfiction, technical writing, and copywriting; some writers focus on certain topics such as health, parenting, travel, and environmental journalism.

Books, magazines, and websites often have market niches, giving writers a chance to specialize in a specific topic. A number of magazines, including *The National Geographic Green Guide, Plenty, Natural Health, Body+Soul,* and *E/The Environmental Magazine,* focus on eco-friendly living and green topics; websites like www.treehugger. com and www.grist.org are devoted to covering environmental subjects.

The BLS reports that more businesses and nonprofit organizations are developing newsletters, websites, and promotional materials. The Sierra Club, World Wildlife Federation, and the Audubon Society publish magazines and maintain websites. Green businesses often hire public relations companies to write press releases, newsletters, and other printed materials to promote their products, providing opportunities for writers to specialize in environmental journalism.

In some cases, writers work regular 9-to-5 shifts. The job might also require working extended hours, including nights and weekends, to meet deadlines. Writers are often able to set their own hours, working on articles, books, and other written materials at almost any time of the day or night. The BLS reports that long and erratic work hours might cause stress, fatigue, or burnout for writers. Using computers for extended periods can also cause health problems such as back pain and eyestrain.

There are over 306,000 writers in the United States. Writers work for advertising agencies, public relations companies, newspapers, magazines, publishing houses, nonprofit organizations, government agencies, and corporations. More than 33 percent work on a freelance or contract basis. Opportunities are expected to increase 10 percent by 2016, especially for writers who produce materials for multimedia clients such as web-based publications.

Writers need a bachelor's degree in journalism, communications, English, or a related field; a master's degree in publishing, journalism, or communications might be required for senior positions.

The American Society of Journalists and Authors (www.asja.org) hosts an annual conference and provides professional resources like job listings and salary reports to its members. Conferences, contests, and career resources are also available to members of the Society of Environmental Journalists (www.sej.org).

The median salary for a writer is $50,660 per year.

Information Technology Consultant

Information technology (IT) consultants manage all computer-related activities within an organization. One of the most important roles an IT consultant has is analyzing technology needs and developing a strategic plan for implementing them. On a daily basis, the responsibilities of this job include installing and upgrading hardware and software, performing programming and systems design, setting up computer networks, implementing Internet and intranet sites, and managing network security. IT consultants are also in charge of managing technical staff such as systems analysts and computer programmers. Some IT consultants work on a contract basis, providing services like custom computer programming, data recovery, and software installation.

IT consultants play a major role in managing energy use and electronics waste. To green IT services within an organization, IT consultants might implement electronics recycling programs for outdated equipment, consolidate servers through *server virtualization*, order energy-efficient equipment such as laptops and *LCD* monitors, and educate computer users about the importance of powering down computers and monitors at the end of the workday.

def•i•ni•tion

Server virtualization is a method of separating one physical server into multiple virtual servers that have the appearance and capabilities of running as their own dedicated machines.

LCD is the acronym for liquid crystal display. LCD monitors are more efficient, use 80 percent less energy, save 520 kWh/year, and eliminate 1,000 pounds of CO_2 emissions than cathode-ray tube monitors.

IT consultants work for corporations, nonprofit organizations, and government agencies; almost all businesses that have computer networks need IT consultants.

Most consultants work 40 hours per week, but evening and weekend work might be required to meet deadlines or address technical issues.

Inside Scoop

The Green Electronics Council (www.greenelectronicscouncil.org) launched the Electronic Product Environmental Assessment Tool, a certification program designed to help IT consultants identify the most eco-friendly computers and monitors on the market. More than 600 products have been certified, and more than 36 million computers have been purchased through the program.

There are 264,000 IT consultants in the United States, and opportunities are expected to increase 16 percent by 2016 as the demand for computer networks, server storage, and other technical solutions continues to grow.

IT consultants need a minimum of a bachelor's degree in computer science, information technology, or a related field. Positions in large corporations or companies with complex technology needs might require candidates to have a master's degree.

IT consultants can attend conferences, take classes, and access professional resources through the Information Technology Association of America (www.itaa.org), the Association of Information Technology Professionals (www.aitp.org), and the Government Electronics and Information Technology Association (www.geia.org).

The median wage for an IT consultant is $101,580 per year.

Florist

Florists design flower arrangements such as bouquets, corsages, and centerpieces using live or dried flowers and greenery. Their job is to select flowers, containers, and other adornments and create attractive arrangements for special events, holidays, weddings, and funerals. Some florists create arrangements for hotels, restaurants, and office buildings.

A growing number of florists are opting to make their flower arrangements more eco-friendly, choosing flowers and greenery that are organic, locally grown, and Fair Trade certified. Florists can also reduce the environmental impact of their arrangements by opting to use vases made from glass or recycled materials instead of plastic, and minimizing the use of balloons, plastic decorations, and other nonrecyclable materials.

The job often entails meeting with customers about their floral and color preferences, budgets, and timelines. Sometimes, orders are taken over the phone. Florists make note of the date the arrangement is needed and where it should be delivered. They must be able to consult with walk-in customers and work quickly to accommodate last-minute orders.

Most florists work in small flower shops where they perform customer service duties and also create floral arrangements. Others may work for online floral retailers or the floral departments in supermarkets. Florists who work for wholesale flower distributors choose flowers to sell to retail florists and create onsite floral displays.

Warning

Florists are susceptible to carpal tunnel syndrome because of the repetitive finger and arm movements required to make floral arrangements. Lifting heavy buckets of flowers and oversized arrangements also puts florists at risk for muscle strain. Florists may also suffer from allergic reactions to certain types of pollen in the flowers they work with on a daily basis.

Most florists learn their skills on-the-job. In fact, florists are the only design professionals who are not required to have formal postsecondary training, according to the BLS. A certificate in floral design from a vocational school or community college can improve employment options. These programs can last from a few weeks up to one year. Some florists opt to earn a bachelor's degree in floriculture or ornamental horticulture.

The American Institute of Floral Designers (AIFD) (www.aifd.org) offers professional accreditation in floral design that signifies a high level of expertise in the field. The exam includes written and design components. The AIFD also hosts national conferences and special events for its members.

There are approximately 87,000 florists in the United States. Approximately 33 percent are self-employed. Opportunities are expected to decline 9 percent by 2016, primarily among florists employed by floral wholesalers due to the large number of flower shops ordering directly from growers.

The median annual salary for a florist is $23,950.

Chapter **13**

Education and Training

In This Chapter

- Undergraduate programs with a green twist
- Growth of the "Green MBA"
- The value of internships in environmental fields
- Where to find the best volunteer opportunities

The number of green careers continues to grow, which means that businesses, nonprofit organizations, and government agencies are in need of qualified candidates to fill those positions. One of the first things employers look for is relevant education and training.

Some green jobs require most of the same skills as their regular counterparts, with a few eco-friendly adjustments that can be learned through on-the-job training. Often, additional certifications are necessary to bolster green knowledge in a specific area. The number of *new* careers created by the green economy has led to a growing demand for candidates who have specific knowledge and experience. The result? New undergraduate and graduate degree programs combined with industry-specific internships and volunteer opportunities designed to arm the next generation of workers with the education and experience to excel in the green economy.

Degree Programs

Many of the most sought-after green careers require job seekers to have a bachelor's degree. Sometimes, you can land a great green career with a degree that's unrelated to the job—a finance major might have a career as a green event manager, and a successful lobbyist might have a degree in English. As competition for green careers grows, though, so does the demand for candidates whose degrees closely match the job descriptions.

New "green degrees" provide students with educations that have clear practical applications in the green economy. Graduates with environmental engineering degrees have the know-how to develop improved forms of recycling, and a degree in sustainable architecture gives a new architect the edge when it comes to designing buildings certified by Leadership in Energy and Environmental Design (LEED). Green degrees give job seekers an edge, and now, more than ever, environmental education is the starting point for Earth-conscious professionals.

Undergraduate Degrees

Almost all colleges and universities offer degrees or majors that could be applied to green careers in various fields; environmental science, biology, botany, chemistry, and geology are just a few examples of programs that provide basic environmental education. Recognizing that students are seeking more specialized programs, a growing number of colleges and universities have begun offering "green degrees" that allow students to focus their attention of specific courses of study related to the growing green economy.

Salt Lake Community College (www.slcc.edu) offers a program in environmental technology that prepares graduates for careers in environmental health, such as hazardous materials cleanup.

The Global Institute of Sustainability at Arizona State University (sustainability.asu.edu) was founded in 2007 to offer sustainability education with a special focus on urban environments. The first class of undergraduate students is expected to top 200, and enrollment in the graduate program is set to double within the first year.

Colorado State University (www.colostate.edu) spent $350,000 to open the School of Global Environmental Sustainability. The school opened in 2008 with the aim of offering its own majors as well as certificate programs in environmental sustainability.

One of its long-term goals is to integrate environmental education into all academic majors, teaching students about technologies that could clean up the planet.

A host of other colleges and universities are also offering degrees in all areas of sustainability. The Rochester Institute of Technology (www.rit.edu) opened a Pollution Prevention Institute to test new environmentally friendly manufacturing methods; Yale Architecture School (www.architecture.yale.edu) offers a degree in sustainable design; and a joint program offered by the National Center for Suburban Studies at Hofstra University (www.hofstra.edu) and Boston College's Urban Ecology Institute (www.bu.edu) is the first program in the nation to focus on suburban ecological and environmental issues.

Lane Community College (www.lanecc.edu) in Eugene, Oregon, offers an associate of applied science degree as a water conservation technician. The program teaches students how to evaluate water use patterns, develop and implement water conservation programs, recommend water efficiency techniques, and perform systems analysis. The first students entered the program in fall 2008.

Dominican University (www.dominican.edu) in San Rafael, California, began offering an undergraduate degree in sustainable communities in 2008 because its master's degree in sustainable enterprise was so popular. The bachelor's degree program allows students to focus on one of two areas—ecological food systems or eco-dwelling, a discipline that examines options for using the sun, wind, and water for shelter and food with a minimal impact on the environment.

A lot of colleges and universities are doing more than just offering green degrees; they're incorporating sustainable practices across their campuses. A school with an eco-friendly campus and amenities such as LEED-certified buildings, a campus-wide composting program, and alternative energy sources ensures that students are getting an environmental education in the classroom and all over campus.

Graduate Degrees

Landing a top-notch green career often means having a top-notch education in the field. Graduate degrees are a must for careers in some of the more competitive fields in the green economy, such as automotive engineer, biofuel research scientist, soil scientist, and investment banker. To get an edge in the green job market, graduate schools are doing more than just offering electives in sustainability; schools are devoting entire master's programs to environmental topics.

The Levin College of Law at the University of Florida (www.ufl.edu) is preparing law graduates to act as environmental advocates with its Master of Laws in Environmental and Land Use Law.

Adelphi University (www.adelphi.edu) in New York, the College of Charleston (www.cofc.edu) in South Carolina, the University of Rhode Island (www.uri.edu), and Columbia University (www.columbia.edu) all offer master's degrees in environmental science.

The most popular graduate programs are "green MBAs," which incorporate traditional business school curricula with classes on climate change, ecological economics, green marketing, and eco-commerce. Dominican University (www.greenmba.com) offers an MBA in sustainable enterprise, Presidio School of Management (www.presidiomba.org) in San Francisco has an MBA program in sustainable management, and an MBA program in sustainable business is offered through Bainbridge Graduate Institute (www.bgiedu.org) on Bainbridge Island, Washington. All three programs have started in the past five years and focus on teaching students about a triple bottom line: profit, people, and planet.

> **Inside Scoop**
>
> Seventy-eight percent of business school students said they wanted classes on corporate social responsibility integrated into core MBA curriculum, according to a survey conducted by Net Impact (www.netimpact.org).

The Aspen Institute Business and Society Program (www.aspeninstitute.org) produces a biennial report that ranks MBA programs around the world on how well they incorporate social and environmental issues into their curriculum. The report, *Beyond Grey Pinstripes* (www.beyondgreypinstripes.org), examines four areas—student opportunities, student exposure, faculty research, and course content—to come up with a list of the top 100 green MBA programs.

Most graduate programs allow students to enroll on a part-time basis, allowing them to pursue an advanced degree while gaining valuable experience in the green economy.

Training

There is no substitute for practical work experience. New graduates and career-changers are often faced with a dilemma: It's hard to find a job without any experience in the field, and it's hard to get experience in the field without a job. So, what's the solution? Sign up for an internship or volunteer work.

Spending a few hours a week—or a few months of the year—learning about a specific green career can make all the difference when it comes to landing a job. Trying a few different fields can also be helpful for making decisions about which career path to follow. Spending time in the field, even without a paycheck, can lead to big payoffs.

Internships

The number of career-related *internships* available for college students is endless. Fields from academia to zoology offer opportunities to get an in-depth look into the career, often by working alongside a professional who can offer insights into what it's really like to have a green job.

def•i•ni•tion _____

Internships are work experiences that provide hands-on experience in a specific career. Most internships are unpaid, but students can often earn college credits for internships related to their majors. Most internships last for a specified period of time, often a semester, and are done in conjunction with college classes.

The number of businesses, nonprofit organizations, and government agencies focusing on the environment makes it easier than ever to find green internships.

National nonprofit organizations are great resources. Take a look at local chapters of the Sierra Club (www.sierraclub.org), Greenpeace (www.greenpeace.org), and the World Wildlife Fund (www.worldwildlife.org) for internship opportunities. College career centers also keep comprehensive lists of employers willing to offer practical work experiences in exchange for college credit, and *The Big Green Internship Book* (www.internships-usa.com/BigGreen/green0506.htm) maintains an up-to-date list of green internships across the United States.

A green degree combined with work experience in a related field will open doors to the best opportunities in the green economy. In fact, over the last year, employers offered full-time jobs to almost two-thirds of their interns, according to a survey conducted by the National Association of Colleges and Employers (www.naceweb.org).

Internships can open the doors to great new careers. However, there are other reasons to sign up for a semester of work experience. Internships can help highlight specific career areas to pursue (and which ones might not be that interesting after all), provide a glimpse into the inner workings of an organization, build a list of valuable contacts, and help earn college credit—making it an incredibly worthwhile experience.

Volunteer Opportunities

Volunteering is a great way to gain experience in a green career. In just a few hours a week, you can have an impact on the environment and gain valuable job skills.

> **Inside Scoop**
>
> More than 60 million Americans volunteer every year, according to the Bureau of Labor Statistics (www.bls.gov), with the majority volunteering 52 hours per year, or approximately one hour per week.

Unlike internships, which are available only to students, volunteer opportunities are open to everyone. Volunteering can be a way to explore a new green career or use the skills gained in a green career to help an organization that needs expertise in a certain field.

Opportunities for volunteers with an interest in the environment are abundant. Websites such as www. volunteermatch.org, www.volunteer.gov, and www. networkforgood.org list volunteer opportunities across the country. Nonprofit organizations like The Nature Conservancy (www. nature.org) and the National Audubon Society (www.audubon.org) also list volunteer opportunities on their websites.

Volunteering isn't all about gaining job skills. For those who love their non-green careers but still want to dedicate time to a green cause, volunteering is a great option. It's also a good way to connect with others who share similar passions and to make a difference in the community—and around the world.

Glossary

air dispersion modeling   A mathematical simulation of how air pollutants disperse in the atmosphere. It is used to estimate the concentration of air pollutants such as factory and vehicle exhaust.

bioenergy   A form of renewable energy made from biological materials that can be used as fuel. The organic matter can be used as fuel or be processed into liquids or gases.

biofuel   A fuel derived from agricultural crops such as sugarcane, corn, and vegetable oil.

biomass   A biological material like corn, switchgrass, or oilseed that can be converted into fuel.

bioremediation   Uses living organisms to clean up contaminated soil or water. Using nitrate and/or sulfate fertilizers to clean up oil spills is one example.

blower doors   Powerful fans that mount on an exterior door and measure the amount of air loss in a building.

brownfield sites   Often former industrial settings that are currently abandoned, vacant, or underutilized because of the presence or potential presence of a hazardous substance, pollutant, or contaminant.

car-sharing programs   Allow members to share a fleet of vehicles that are located throughout a community. Members can borrow cars for short periods of time, often by the hour, without any of the expenses of car ownership, like maintenance and insurance.

carbon audits Used to measure the carbon footprints of organizations for the purposes of carbon emissions trading.

carbon footprint Measures the amount of carbon dioxide and other greenhouse gases emitted by a person, corporation, or lifecycle of a product or service.

Clean Air Act Sets limits on how much of a pollutant can be present in the air.

Clean Water Act Enacts standards for water pollution, including reducing water pollution from industrial facilities, governments, and agricultural operations.

CO_2 cleaning A method of dry cleaning that cleans clothes using nontoxic liquid CO_2.

community gardens These rent garden shares to members, allowing them to grow fruits, vegetables, and flowers on public land while sharing resources with other members.

community-supported agriculture (CSA) Also called *subscription farming*, it allows members to purchase shares in a local farm in exchange for regular, often weekly, deliveries of farm products such as fruits, herbs, flowers, nuts, eggs, milk, and meat during the growing season.

compact fluorescent light bulbs (CFLs) These use 75 percent less energy than standard incandescent bulbs and last up to 10 times longer.

compost A nutrient-rich soil substance that is created when organic waste, like food scraps and grass clippings, decomposes.

eco-tourism Refers to responsible travel to natural areas that conserves the environment and improves the well-being of local people.

emission reduction credits Granted upon request to companies that reduce their emissions below required levels. Extra credits can be bought, sold, or traded.

emissions tests The measurement of hydrocarbons, nitrogen oxide, carbon monoxide, carbon dioxide, and evaporative emissions released by a car.

ENERGY STAR A program managed by the U.S. Environmental Protection Agency (EPA) and the Department of Energy (DOE) that designates high-efficiency products.

energy-efficient mortgages   Also called *green mortgages*, these offer lower interest rates or rebates to borrowers who purchase new energy-efficient homes, invest in energy-efficient retrofits, or purchase green power.

fisheries   Established areas where fish species, including shellfish, are raised and caught. They are also called *aquaculture farms*.

Forest Stewardship Council   Provides certification that wood comes from certified and well-managed forests; its standards have been applied in 57 countries around the world.

franchises   National companies with established customer bases and methods of conducting business. Franchisees enter into contracts to use the franchise name on a nonexclusive basis to sell goods or services.

fuel economy   Measures how efficiently a vehicle converts fuel into useful performance. In the United States, fuel economy is calculated in miles per gallon.

geothermal energy   Generated by heat stored beneath the surface of the earth, it can also find its way to the surface through volcanoes, hot springs, and geysers.

geothermal heat pumps   These use a network of buried pipes that are linked to a heat exchanger and ductwork to transfer heat in and out of buildings.

green roofs   Rooftop gardens filled with plants like sedum, wildflowers, and native grasses. They reduce air pollution and stormwater runoff, mitigate noise, and act as wildlife habitats.

greenhouse gas   Made up of gases such as carbon dioxide, methane, nitrous oxide, and ozone that are present in the atmosphere and that contribute to global warming.

heat island effect   Refers to the increase in temperature that occurs over large paved areas, especially in big cities. Natural areas such as forests, parks, and wetlands help to minimize the heat island effect.

high-emissivity materials   Help curb excess heat gain by reflecting radiant solar energy. The result is less energy required for heating and cooling.

hydroelectric power   The electrical energy produced by flowing water. It produces no waste or carbon dioxide—a common greenhouse gas—and is the most widely used source of renewable energy.

infrared cameras   Used to reveal hard-to-detect areas of air infiltration.

integrated pest management (IPM)   An environmentally sensitive approach to pest management that aims to reduce and/or eliminate the use of pesticides.

integrated solid waste management   Refers to the process of minimizing the amount of waste that ends up in landfills through waste prevention, composting, and recycling with minimal impact on the environment.

Kyoto Protocol   A United Nations treaty designed to reduce greenhouse gas emissions worldwide. It was adopted in 1997 and signed and ratified by 182 parties around the world.

Leadership in Energy and Environmental Design (LEED)   A voluntary, consensus-based national standard enacted by the U.S. Green Building Council for the design, construction, and operation of high-performance, sustainable buildings.

Leadership in Energy and Environmental Design Accredited Professionals (LEED APs)   Certified through the U.S. Green Building Certification Institute as professionals who have demonstrated a thorough understanding of green building practices and principles and the LEED rating system.

Leave No Trace   Encourages the responsible enjoyment of outdoor recreation areas with minimal impact on the environment.

light-emitting diode (LED)   A bulb that produces more light per watt than an incandescent bulb. LEDs are often used in traffic signals, cameras, and telephone dials.

lignocellulosic biomass   Plant biomass composed of cellulose or lignin, such as sawmill discards, municipal paper waste, agricultural residues like sugarcane, and tall grasses, that is converted to ethanol through fermentation.

microbreweries   Breweries that produce fewer than 15,000 barrels of beer per year.

mutual funds   A managed group of investments in stocks, bonds, and other securities. The fund combines money from thousands of small investors, each of which owns shares in the fund.

National Association of Securities Dealers Automated Quotation System (NASDAQ)   The largest screen-based equity securities trading market in the United States, it lists more than 3,200 companies.

royal jelly   A glandular secretion produced by young bees that is high in vitamin B, amino acids, unsaturated fats, and minerals. It is a natural ingredient used in dietary supplements and beauty products.

server virtualization   A method of separating one physical server into multiple virtual servers that have the appearance and capabilities of running as their own dedicated machines.

socially responsible investing (SRI)   Refers to an investment strategy that maximizes financial return by investing in companies that promote corporate best practices such as environmental stewardship, human rights, and diversity.

solar power   Converts the radiant energy of the sun into electricity.

stormwater   The flow of water that results from precipitation such as rain and snow. Stormwater soaks into the surface of the soil, saturates plants, and evaporates into the atmosphere. The stormwater that remains becomes runoff and causes erosion of land area and stream banks, increases flooding, and carries pollutants to surface waters. Increased development destroys natural areas and results in more runoff.

sustainable urban development   Aims to improve the long-term social and environmental health of cities. It includes compact land use, improved access to public transportation, efficient resource use, decreased pollution and waste, restoration of the natural environment, sustainable economics, preservation of local culture, and community involvement.

volatile organic compounds (VOCs)   The chemicals found in paint and stains that release harmful pollutants into the atmosphere.

wet cleaning   A method of dry cleaning that uses water and specialized detergents instead of harsh chemicals in computer-controlled washers and dryers. The process generates no hazardous waste or air pollution and reduces the potential for water and soil contamination.

wind farms   Plots of land with several wind turbines that are used for the production of electric power.

wind turbines   Rotating machines that generate mechanical power. The mechanical power can be channeled through a generator and converted into electricity.

Resources

Here, all in one place, is a comprehensive list of the essential books, web-sites, and conferences that you'll need to start your search for a green career.

Books

Building the Green Economy: Success Stories from the Grassroots by Kevin Danaher, Shannon Biggs, and Jason Mark, Poilpoint Press, 2007.

Careers in the Environment by Mike Fasulo and Paul Walker, McGraw-Hill Companies, 2007.

Careers in Renewable Energy: Get a Green Energy Job by Gregory McNamee, Pixy-Jack Press, 2008.

Careers for Environmental Types and Others Who Respect the Earth by Mike Fasulo and Paul Walker, McGraw-Hill Companies, 2001.

The Eco-Guide to Careers That Make a Difference: Environmental Work for A Sustainable World by Environmental Careers Organization, Island Press, 2004.

Environmental Careers in the 21ˢᵗ Century by Environmental Careers Organization, Island Press, 1999.

Ethical Markets: Growing the Green Economy by Hazel Henderson and Simran Sethi, Chelsea Green, 2007.

Great Jobs for Environmental Studies Majors, Second Edition, by Julie DeGalan, McGraw-Hill, 2008.

Green Careers by Frank Marquardt, wetfeet.com, 2008.

Green Careers: Choosing Work for a Sustainable Future by Jim Cassio and Alice Rush, New Society Publishers, 2009.

Green Jobs: A Guide to Eco-Friendly Employment by A. Bronwyn Llewellyn, M.A.; James P. Hendrix, Ph.D.; and K.C. Golden, M.A., Adams Media, 2008.

Green Volunteers: The World Guide to Voluntary Work in Nature Conservation, by Fabio Ausenda, ed., Universe Publishing, 2005.

Making a Living While Making a Difference by Melissa Everett, New Society, 2007.

Saving the Earth as a Career: Advice on Becoming a Conservation Professional by Malcolm L. Hunter, Jr.; David Lindenmayer; and Aram Calhoun, Wiley-Blackwell, 2007.

Websites

Business for Social Responsibility
www.bsr.org/jobs/csr
An organization that works with businesses to promote a more sustainable world. Includes research on business development and environmental issues, and information about annual conferences.

Eco.org
www.eco.org
A one-stop shop for all things eco-friendly, from products and services to job listings.

EcoEmploy
www.ecoemploy.com
Links to green jobs in the United States and Canada.

EnviroNetwork
www.environetwork.com
Listings for green jobs, separated by industry.

Environmental Career Opportunities
www.ecojobs.com
Postings for green jobs in fields ranging from outdoor education and environmental advocacy to renewable energy and environmental policy. Also includes a section for international opportunities.

EnvironmentalCareer.com
www.environmentalcareer.com
Site connects green job seekers to leading environmental employers across the United States.

EnvironmentalJobs.com

www.environmentaljobs.com

Comprehensive listing of jobs in environmental fields. Weekly e-newsletter includes e-mail delivery of the latest job listings.

Green Energy Jobs

www.greenenergyjobs.com

International job site for renewable energy industries. Includes listings for all areas of the renewable energies sector, such as wind, carbon, solar, and bioenergy.

Green Jobs

www.greenjobs.com

Listings for jobs in the renewable energy industries in North America and abroad. Also offers the latest industry news and an e-newsletter, MonsterTRAK.

green-jobs.monstertrak.com

Site devoted to green jobs, powered by Monster.com. Includes listings in the United States and abroad.

GreenBiz.com

www.greenbiz.com/jobs

Postings for jobs that emphasize the environment, and sustainable business practices.

SimplyHired

www.simplyhired.com

Job listings by category. No specific section for green jobs, but categories such as biotech, nonprofit, and engineering often contain postings for green jobs.

SustainableBusiness.com

www.sustainablebusiness.com

Global news and networking opportunities for sustainable businesses. Also includes a link to "Green Dream Jobs" with listings across the United States.

Treehugger

www.treehugger.com

News, events, and reviews with an environmental bent. Site also includes a job board.

Grist.org

jobs.grist.org

Leading environmental site lists green jobs along with environmental news and commentary.

Orion Society

www.oriongrassroots.org

Connects grassroots groups with environmental missions. Includes event listings, resources, and a job board.

GuideStar
www.guidestar.org
Comprehensive listing of jobs in the nonprofit sector, including careers in environmental fields.

Idealist.org
www.idealist.org
Site focuses on issues of interest to nonprofit organizations and job seekers. Includes listings for green careers with not-for-profits.

Conferences

Bioneers Conference
www.bioneers.org

Clean Technology and Sustainable Industries Conference and Trade Show
www.ct-si.org

Geothermal Energy Association Conference
www.geo-energy.org

Good Jobs, Green Jobs: A National Green Jobs Conference
www.greenjobsconference.org

Green Business Conference
www.coopamerica.org/greenbusiness/conference.cfm

Green Festival
www.coopamerica.org/greenbusiness/greenfestivals.cfm

Greenbuild International Conference and Expo
www.greenbuildexpo.org

Solar Living Institute Green Careers Conference
www.solarliving.org

Solar Power Conference
www.solarpowerconference.com

WindPower Expo
www.windpowerexpo.org

Certifications for Green Job Seekers

The growth in the green economy has created a wealth of new careers and changed the job duties in existing occupations. As a result, a host of new certification programs has cropped up to address the need for workers with green skills. This appendix provides a comprehensive reference list that includes all of the certifications listed in each chapter.

Chapter 2: Environment

American League of Lobbyists
www.alldc.org

Association of Fundraising Professionals
www.afpnet.org

Center for Nonprofit Management
www.cnm.org

International Association of Business Communicators
www.iabc.com

The Public Relations Society of America
www.prsa.org

Water Quality Association
www.wqa.org

Chapter 3: Green Building

American Council for Construction Education
www.acce-hq.org

American Institute of Certified Planners
www.planning.org/aicp

American Nursery & Landscape Association
www.anla.org

American Society for Testing and Materials
www.astm.org

Associated Schools of Construction
www.ascweb.org

Association of Energy Engineers
www.aeecenter.org

BuiltGreen
www.builtgreen.net

Council of Landscape Architectural Registration Boards
www.clarb.org

Green Building Certification Institute
www.gbci.org

Green Roofs for Healthy Cities
www.greenroofs.org

GreenAdvantage
www.greenadvantage.org

International Code Council
www.iccsafe.org

International Society of Arboriculture
www.isa-arbor.com

National Association of Home Builders
www.nahb.org

National Council of Architectural Registration Boards
www.ncarb.org

National Kitchen & Bath Association
www.nkba.org

National Insulation Association
www.insulation.org

National Sustainable Building Advisor Program
www.nasbap.org

Residential Energy Services Network
www.resnet.us

Tree Care Industry Association
www.tcia.org

U.S. Environmental Protection Agency
www.epa.gov

Chapter 4: Renewable Energy

American Society of Heating, Refrigerating and Air-Conditioning Engineers
www.ashrae.org

American Welding Society
www.aws.org

Institute of Electrical and Electronics Engineers
www.ieee.org

Laramie County Community College
www.lccc.cc.wy.us

North American Board of Certified Energy Practitioners
www.nabcep.org

Sheet Metal and Air Conditioning Industry
www.sheetmetal-iti.org

Chapter 5: Natural Resources

American Fisheries Society
www.fisheries.org

American Institute of Hydrology
www.aihydrology.org

Association of National Park Rangers
www.anpr.org

Global Restoration Network
www.globalrestorationnetwork.org

Marine Stewardship Council
www.msc.org

National Recreation and Park Association
www.nrpa.org

Society for Ecological Restoration International
www.ser.org

Society of American Foresters
www.safnet.org

Chapter 6: Sustainable Agriculture

American Fisheries Society
www.fisheries.org

American Society of Agronomy
www.agronomy.org

American Society of Farm Managers and Rural Appraisers
www.asfmra.org

California Certified Organic Farmers
www.ccof.org

Crop Science Society of America
www.crops.org

Independent Organic Inspectors Association
www.ioia.net

Institute of Food Technologists
www.ift.org

IPM Institute of North America
www.ipminstitute.org

National Association of State Departments of Agriculture
www.nasda.org

Society for Range Management
www.rangelands.org

Soil Science Society of America
www.soils.org

United States Department of Agriculture
www.usda.gov

United States Department of Agriculture National Organic Standards Program
www.ams.usda.gov

Chapter 7: Waste Management

American Academy of Environmental Engineers
www.aaee.net

American Indoor Air Quality Council
www.iaqcouncil.org

American Meteorological Society
www.ametsoc.org

Association of Energy Engineers
www.aeecenter.org

Greenhouse Gas Management Institute
www.ghginstitute.org

Indoor Air Quality Association
www.iaqa.org

International Indoor Air Quality Commission
www.iiaqc.org

National Association of Remediators and Mold Inspectors
www.normi.org

Occupational Safety and Health Administration (OSHA)
www.osha.gov

WERC
www.werc.net

Chapter 8: Facilities Management

Architectural Testing
www.archtest.com

Association of Energy Engineers
www.aeecenter.org

Association of Higher Education Facilities
www.appa.org

Building Performance Institute
www.bpi.org

International Facility Management Association
www.ifma.org

National Energy Management Institute
www.nemionline.org

North American Technician Excellence
www.natex.org

Professional Grounds Management Society
www.pgms.org

Chapter 9: Transportation

American Institute of Constructors
www.aicnet.org

American Marketing Association
www.marketingpower.com

American Society for Quality
www.asq.org

Automotive Service Association
www.asashop.org

Automotive Training Centres
www.autotrainingcentre.com

Construction Management Association of America
www.cmaanet.org

Fabricators & Manufacturers Association, International
www.fmanet.org

Institute of Transportation Engineers
www.ite.org

International Organization for Standardization
www.iso.org

National Institute for Automotive Service Excellence
www.ase.com

Public Relations Society of America
www.prsa.org

Society of Automotive Engineers
www.sae.org

U.S. Federal Communications Commission
www.fcc.gov

Chapter 10: Financial Services

Bank Administration Institute
www.bai.org

Certified Financial Planner Board of Standards
www.cfp.net

CFA Institute
www.cfainstitute.org

Financial Industry Regulatory Authority
www.finra.org

Greenhouse Gas Management Institute
www.ghginstitute.org

Mortgage Bankers Association
www.mbaa.org

North American Securities Administration Association
www.nasaa.org

Chapter 11: Business and Hospitality Services

American Culinary Federation
www.acfchefs.org

American Hotel & Lodging Association
www.ahla.com

American Society of Travel Agents
www.asta.org

Convention Industry Council
www.conventionindustry.org

Green Meeting Industry Council
www.greenmeetings.info

Green Seal
www.greenseal.org

National Business Travel Association
www.nbta.org

National Tour Association
www.ntaonline.com

Society of Government Meeting Professionals
www.sgmp.org

Sustainable Travel International
www.sustainabletravelinternational.org

Chapter 12: Small Business Opportunities

EcoBroker International
www.ecobroker.com

Professional Landcare Network
www.landcarenetwork.org

Chapter 13: Education and Training

Adelphi University
www.adelphi.edu

The Aspen Institute Business and Society Program
www.aspeninstitute.org

Bainbridge Graduate Institute
www.bgiedu.org

Boston College's Urban Ecology Institute
www.bu.edu

College of Charleston
www.cofc.edu

Colorado State University
www.colostate.edu

Columbia University
www.columbia.edu

Dominican University of California
www.dominican.edu

The Global Institute for Sustainability at Arizona State University
sustainability.asu.edu

Hofstra University's National Center for Suburban Studies
www.hofstra.edu

Lane Community College
www.lanecc.edu

Presidio School of Management
www.presidiomba.org

The Rochester Institute of Technology
www.rit.edu

Salt Lake Community College
www.slcc.edu

University of Florida, Levin College of Law
www.ufl.edu

University of Rhode Island
www.uri.edu

Yale School of Architecture
www.architecture.yale.edu

Index